A Pictorial Panorama of Early Russian Methodism

1889 – 1931

by

S T Kimbrough, Jr.

Copyright © 2009 General Commission on Archives and History
The United Methodist Church
36 Madison Avenue
P.O. Box 127
Madison, New Jersey 07940

No part of this book may be reproduced or transmitted in any form or by any means, electronic or mechanical, including photocopying, recording, or by any information storage and retrieval system, without permission in writing from the publisher.

A Pictorial Panorama of Early Russian Methodism
by
S T Kimbrough, Jr.

Cover design by
Mark Starr Kimbrough

ISBN 978-1-880927-22-9

Manufactured in the United States of America

Contents

Foreword   Bishop Hans Växby   iv

Preface   S T Kimbrough, Jr.   v

The Methodist Episcopal Church
Beginnings   1
St. Petersburg and Surrounding Area   14
Publications   15
Registration   20
The Methodist Episcopal Church Russia Mission Grows   24
The Role of the Baltic States   33
Baltic and Slavic Mission Conference   39
The Deaconess Movement   42
Conclusion   44

The Methodist Episcopal Church, South
The Siberia-Manchuria Mission   45
Russian Siberia   46
Vladivostok and the Primorski Krai Region   50
The Missionaries   51
Russian-Language Work in Harbin, China   54
The First Indigenous Russian Pastors in Harbin   62
Women's Work   65
Publications   66
The Closing of the Mission   70
Report of V. N. Pestrikoff   73
Epilogue   75

Appendix 1: Biographical Statements of the Bishops of the Missions
A. The Methodist Episcopal Church   77
B. The Methodist Episcopal Church, South   79

Appendix 2: Gallery of Additional Photos from the Missions
A. The Methodist Episcopal Church   81
B. The Methodist Episcopal Church, South   85

Appendix 3: Additional Photos of Students Preparing for Ministry   95

Appendix 4: Methodist Episcopal Church, South and White Russia   98

Index of Personal Names   100

About the Author   104

Foreword

In 1992 I was bishop of the Nordic and Baltic Episcopal area of The United Methodist Church and in August of that year I traveled to Moscow to attend the organizational meeting of The United Methodist Mission in the Commonwealth of Independent States, i.e. eleven former Soviet republics. It was, within a few days, precisely one hundred years after the organization of the Methodist Episcopal Mission in Finland and St. Petersburg. Present at this gathering also was a young man from St. Petersburg, Andrei Pupko. He represented a number of house churches created by a British Methodist evangelist, which were considering joining the new United Methodist connection.

During one of the presentations he heard for the first time the history of Methodism in Russia. In the break, he rushed to a public telephone and called his friends back home. He wanted them immediately to know, "We are not the first Methodists in town. One hundred years ago they were already there!"

This is an experience I wish for United Methodists and their friends in Russia, Ukraine, Belarus, Moldova, and Central Asia: Methodists have a history in Russia and among Russian-speaking people. This book provides an opportunity for people to see and encounter the faces, places, and facts of early Russian Methodism. I am sure that those who read it will marvel at the grace of God, and be inspired to be faithful and brave in today's ministry.

Dr. S T Kimbrough, Jr., has created a unique document. He is the scholar *par excellence* of early Russian Methodism. This book is an invaluable gift to The United Methodist Church in Eurasia, celebrating its 120th anniversary of the beginning of Methodist work in Russia and the 100th anniversary of the official registration of the Methodist Episcopal Church on June 12, 1909.

Hans Växby,
Bishop of the Eurasia Area
The United Methodist Church

Preface

This book does not attempt an exhaustive history of early Methodism in Russia; rather it brings together photographs and documents this author first collected as part of the research for the volume *Methodism in Russia and the Baltic States: History and Renewal*.[1] Of course, some materials have come to light since then and are also included. No doubt others are yet to be discovered.

There are two major parts to a multifaceted story of the beginnings and growth of Methodism in Russia proper, in Russian Siberia, among the Russian-speaking emigrant communities of China (Manchuria), and in the Baltic States. The two major parts have to do with the mission efforts in the early twentieth century of two branches of Methodism, the Methodist Episcopal Church[2] and the Methodist Episcopal Church, South,[3] which united with the Methodist Protestant Church in 1939 to form The Methodist Church.

The mission work of the MEC began in the 1880s in and around St. Petersburg, Russia, and it was intimately related to the development of Methodism in the Baltic States, which began ca. 1900 in Kaunas, Lithuania. The labor and untiring efforts of the Rev. Dr. George A. Simons, the Rev. Hjalmar Salmi, and Sister Anna Eklund are inspiring ones to retell today. The development of congregations, orphanages, humanitarian aid, and theological training of ministers were integral facets of the MEC Mission.

Some of the Russian-language documents discovered in my early research, which verify the official registration of the MEC in Russia, appear in print here for the first time.

The Siberia-Manchuria Mission was opened by the MECS and at the outset was primarily outreach to emigrant Koreans, largely farmers, who had fled north into Russian Siberia and the Chinese North Kondo region before and after the Japanese invasion of the Korean peninsula in 1910. A number of Korean MEC congregations and schools for children were founded, e.g. in Vladivostok and Nikolsk-Ussurisk. The Mission, however, also began work among the Russians, primarily in Vladivostok.

The final takeover of Russian Siberia by the Bolsheviks was not realized until the fall of 1922. The difficulties created by them led the MECS mission officials to close the Mission in Russian Siberia and move all mission personnel and programs to Harbin, China, where there were large Russian and Korean emigrant populations. The growth of Methodism among the Russians of Harbin is an amazing story of the rapid development of educational and medical institutions, churches, ministerial training, and humanitarian aid.

The periods covered in this volume are as follows:
    1. Missions of the MEC to Russia proper (1880s to 1931)[4]
    2. Missions of the MEC to the Baltic States (1900 to 1939)
    3. Siberia-Manchuria Mission of the MEC (1920 to 1927)

The missions of the MEC in the Baltic States are addressed in this volume to some extent, since they are directly and indirectly related to the work of the MEC in Russia. At the time of the birth of Methodism in Russia and the Baltic States, namely, the end of the nineteenth and

---

[1] Nashville: Abingdon Press, 1995.

[2] Cited henceforth as MEC.

[3] Cited henceforth as MECS.

[4] Though the Russian city of St. Petersburg has other names in various periods of history, e.g., Leningrad and Petrograd, it is referred to in this volume only by the name of St. Petersburg.

the beginning of the twentieth centuries respectively, the Baltic States were a part of Imperial Russia. Primarily those aspects of Methodism in the Baltic States that are related to the MEC in Russia proper and Russian-language ministries are treated here. Since the Russian-speaking Methodist congregations in Estonia were not begun until 1957, after the return of the Rev. Alexander Kuum from imprisonment in Siberia, they are not discussed in this volume.

So far as the Siberia-Manchuria Mission of the MECS is concerned, one must address both Korean[5] and Russian ministries. The pictographic material related to the Korean mission in Siberia used in this volume is primarily from Vladivostok and Nikolsk-Ussurisk. The concentration of photographs from Harbin available to this author have to do with Russian-language ministries. Nevertheless, it must be emphasized that in Harbin there were Japanese, Korean, Chinese, and Russian MECS churches. The amazing growth and breadth of Korean-language ministries of the Siberia-Manchuria Mission in the North Kondo region of China and Harbin has yet to be properly explored and deserves an appropriate place in Methodist mission history.

The author expresses deep appreciation to the Rev. Dr. Robert Williams, General Secretary of the General Commission on Archives and History of The United Methodist Church, and to the staff of the Commission at Drew University, L. Dale Patterson (Archivist/Records Administrator) and Mark C. Shenise (Associate Archivist) for their extraordinary and vital assistance in procuring many of the photographs which appear in this volume. Sincere gratitude is also expressed to Irina Miagkova for the English translation of some Russian documents, and to Mark Starr Kimbrough for the cover design. I am also grateful to the Rev. Gita Mednis (Latvia) and the Rev. Taavi Holman (Estonia) for assistance with a number of names and photographs, Wilfried Nausner (Austria) for information regarding the MECS and White Russia, the Rev. Charles A. Green for assistance with technical matters, the Rev. Dr. David C. Wu for Mandarin translation, and Eunice Brown, daughter of the Rev. and Mrs. George F. Erwin, the last missionaries of the MECS assigned to Russian Siberia, who provided the author with valuable photographs of the life, work, and people of the Siberia-Manchuria Mission.

This publication is made possible through the gift of Frederick E. Maser and Mary Louise Jarden Maser.

The photographs in this volume are of varying quality. Most are from the early part of the twentieth century. Some have been well preserved, while others are in poor condition. Some have been created by scanning pages of magazines and publications of the period. No doubt the photographs and documents included here are but a miniscule part of the whole story of early Russian Methodism, but it is sincerely hoped that they will reveal the passion and commitment of those who labored so diligently for Christ and the church, while often suffering greatly. May they never be forgotten!

S T Kimbrough, Jr.,
Research Fellow
Center for Studies in the Wesleyan Tradition
The Divinity School
Durham, North Carolina

---

[5] Since this volume is about early Russian Methodism, it includes the MECS Korean congregations in the Russian territory of Siberia (Primorski Krai). While the Siberia-Manchuria Mission of the MECS included many Korean congregations in the North Kondo region of China (near Russian Siberia), they are not addressed here.

The Methodist Episcopal Church
Beginnings

The story of the birth and history of Methodism in Russia is very complex. The general outline of the story can be documented and, as Methodism grew in Russia and neighboring countries, the evidence becomes stronger and stronger. While I have told the story elsewhere in the book, *Methodism in Russia and the Baltic States: History and Renewal* (1995), the photographs in this volume connect the reader with the people and places that give life to the story in a very different way from the prose narrative.

The story of the beginnings of Methodism in Russia must be understood in a broader context than merely the geographically restricted area of Russia proper, since it unfolds during the final years of Tsarist Russia when the Romanoffs were still in power and the imperial empire included vast regions from the Baltic Sea to the Far East to Crimea in the south and Ukraine in the west. The Baltic states of Estonia, Latvia, and Lithuania, then part of the Russian Empire, are extremely important for the story of early Russian Methodism, since these states have a significant role in its birth and growth in the Empire.

Scandinavian Methodism had an important part in the birth of Methodism on Russian soil. In 1866, the Bärnlund brothers, who had been converted on the Methodist Episcopal Church Bethel ship "John Wesley" in the New York harbor, returned to their native Finland with the Christian message and the story of Methodism. Three years later the Rev. Bengt A. Carlson, an American of Swedish birth, was sent to open Methodist work in Sweden. By the 1870s two Swedish lay preachers, C. Martinson and Karl Lindborg, had begun to evangelize throughout their homeland and Finland. By 1881/1882, Lindborg traveled to St. Petersburg for the first time and preached there to Swedish-speaking residents. There were significant Swedish and Finnish populations in and around St. Petersburg with an opportunity to evangelize. It does not appear, however, that congregations were formally organized at that time. Nevertheless, seeds were sown for the growth of Methodism in Russia.

In 1888, the Rev. Bengt A. Carlson was invited to preach in Russia and in May of the following year began monthly evangelizations in St. Petersburg. In August 1889, he rented a meeting hall and on September 17th preached his first sermon there. The following November a small Methodist congregation was organized. Because of lack of funds, however, Carlson had to abandon the rented hall in 1890. In 1891 he returned to Sweden after the death of his wife, but in 1902 he went back to St. Petersburg.

In April 1905 the Edict of Toleration was issued by Tsar Nicholas II and became extremely important for early Methodist history in Russia, for it granted religious minorities the right to exist under Russian law. It is here that the story of Methodism's birth on Russian soil turns to another part of the Tsarist Russian Empire, namely, Lithuania.

Toward the end of the nineteenth century a strong evangelical movement swept across the Baltic states. At this time a small group of faithful Lutherans in Kaunas, Lithuania, who sought a deeper spirituality in the life of prayer, Bible study, fellowship, and sharing, made contact with the MEC in Germany (*bischöfliche methodistische Kirche*). In 1900 German Methodist pastor, the Rev. Heinrich Ramke of Königsberg, visited them in Kaunas and they immediately identified with the Wesleyan way of spirituality Ramke shared with them and expressed the desire to become Methodists. The following year, 1901, Bishop John Nuelsen recognized the congregation, and four years later (1905) a pastor, the Rev. Georg Durdis, from the Northern

German Methodist Conference, was assigned to Kaunas. The same year, 1905, Nicholas II, Tsar of Russia, issued the Edit of Toleration, which guaranteed religious freedom throughout the Russian Empire and became part of the new Russian constitution. Though the congregation in Kaunas applied for official recognition by the Russian government in 1901, and to hold services according to the Methodist tradition, the request was denied. This did not deter the Kaunas congregation, which was determined to become active in the larger Methodist connection and communities of faith.

By 1906, when the congregation once again made the same request, it was granted. The Russian-language document cited below and dated April 12, 1906, officially granted permission to the Kaunas congregation to conduct Methodist worship services. This, of course transpired during the year following the Edict of Toleration (1905).

Georg Durdis

Two documents follow which reflect the congregation's efforts to be recognized by the government. Copies of the original documents follow the English translations.

The Ministry of Internal Affairs
Governor Norensky
Dec. 29th, 1905
Kaunas City

To General Governor of Vilnius, Kaunas, and Grodno:

The followers of Methodist faith residing in the Šciančia Settlement of Kaunas region and immediate surroundings apply for permission to perform worship according to traditions of their faith and to have their own house of worship with a preacher.

Collected information demonstrates that—the followers of the Methodist faith reside in the settlement of Šciančia, town of Kaunas, and the settlement of Aleksota of Suvalkskoy province; do not differ in their way of life or occupations from residents who belong to other faiths; work in the factories of Schmitt and Tillmans, and are (were) in sales; are of excellent behavior, and have neither been nor are on trial or under investigation.

A similar application had been put forth by the aforementioned Methodists in 1901, but the Ministry of Internal Affairs, according to guidelines on foreign faiths issued by the Department of Spiritual Affairs on September 25, 1901 (document #4307), instructed the former governor of Kaunas to inform the applicants that their application to perform worship according to traditions of their sect and to have their own house of worship with an appointed preacher has been recognized as unworthy of attention and will be left without follow-up.

Submitting this application for your High Excellency's consideration, I report that since one cannot find anything objectionable in the Methodists' way of life or in their teachings, then I, from my point of view, do not see any obstacles to the positive resolution of their application.

Attached please find a list of the followers of the Methodist Sect and the main rules of their faith.

Signed,
Vice Governor

Ministry of Internal Affairs
Department of Religious Matters of Foreign Affairs
April 12, 1906
No. 639

To: The Chancellery of the Vilnius, Kaunas, and Grodno Governor General:

Receipt stamps:
Chancellery of the Vilnius Governor General, April 20, 1906
Chancellery of the Governor General, Department III: Incoming No. 678

    In his letter No. 636, of January 28 last, the Vilnius, Kaunas, and Grodno Governor advised this Ministry of a petition by the followers of the Methodist doctrine residing in the Village of Šiančia, Kaunas parish, who requested that they be allowed to conduct worship services according to the rites of their faith and granted permission to set up in that village a house of worship with an appointed preacher.
    The records of this Department indicate that said petitioners had addressed their petition directly to the Ministry of Internal Affairs in October last, 1905, at which time they also requested that the preacher of their community also be made responsible for keeping the books of civic records for members thereof. Upon reviewing said petition, the Ministry found that the confession of the Methodist sect has not been duly recognized within the borders of the Empire and that, for this reason, the question of allowing at the present time the activities of the sect on an equal basis with those of other non-Orthodox faiths that are recognized in Russia is *ipso facto* subject to a negative decision. However, taking into consideration that, pursuant to Article 45 of the Basic State Law, the freedom of confession is granted not only to Christians of foreign faiths, but even to Jews, Moslems, and Pagans, and that Methodists, judging by the exposition of the rules of their faith presented by them, adhere to a religious teaching that instructs its members to obey the supreme authorities in the country of their residence and its laws, the Ministry, in its Letter No. 5656 of January 14 last, advised the Kaunas Governor that, in the light of the IMPERIAL Manifesto of October 17, 1905, it finds no obstacle to permitting the followers of said sect to conduct worship meetings in said village, while solely making the police responsible for oversight to ensure that no activities contrary to good morals and public order take place in the meetings of these sectarians. As to the petition of said persons concerning the creation of a house of worship and appointment of a special preacher for them, such petition could not be satisfied prior to a legislative passage of the rules that will define the procedures for formation and the modes of activity of the various communities belonging to those Christian faiths that are not provided for by the laws currently in effect, to which I deem it necessary to add that the Department of Religious Matters of Foreign Affairs has already commended the drafting of such rules and that, in this endeavor, the request of said petitioners concerning arrangements for the keeping of their civic records will be given due consideration.

                                                    Director [signature]

№ 17

МИНИСТЕРСТВО
ВНУТРЕННИХЪ ДѢЛЪ.
КОВЕНСКАГО
ГУБЕРНАТОРА.

По Губернскому Правленію.

24 Декабря 190 5 го.

№ ____

Г. Ковна.

Виленскому, Ковенскому и Гродненскому
Генералъ-Губернатору.

Послѣдователи методистскаго вѣроученія, проживающіе въ селеніи Шанцахъ, Ковенскаго уѣзда, и ближайшихъ окрестностяхъ, ходатайствуютъ о разрѣшеніи имъ отправлять богослуженіе по обрядамъ своей вѣры и имѣть свой молитвенный домъ съ особымъ проповѣдникомъ.

Изъ собранныхъ свѣдѣній видно, что послѣдователи методистскаго ученія проживаютъ въ селеніи Шанцахъ, гор. Ковнѣ и посадѣ Алексотѣ, Сувалкской губерніи; по образу жизни и занятіямъ они ничѣмъ не отличаются отъ жителей другихъ вѣроисповѣданій, работаютъ на заводахъ Тильманса и нѣкоторые изъ нихъ занимаются торговлей; поведенія они безукоризненнаго, подъ судомъ и слѣдствіемъ не состояли и не состоятъ.

Подобное ходатайство возбуждено было означенными методистами въ 1901г., но Министерство Внутреннихъ Дѣлъ, въ предложеніи по Департаменту Духовныхъ Дѣлъ Иностранныхъ Исповѣданій отъ 25 сентября 1901г. за № 4827, увѣдомило бывшаго Ковенскаго Губернатора, для объявленія просителямъ, что ходатайство ихъ о разрѣшеніи отправлять богослуженіе по обрядамъ ихъ секты и устроить молитвенный домъ съ назначеніемъ къ нему особаго проповѣдника признано Министерствомъ не заслуживающимъ уваженія и оставлено безъ послѣдствій.

Представляя настоящее ходатайство методистовъ

ныхъ исповѣданій, но и евреямъ, магометанамъ и язычникамъ, и что методисты, судя по представленному ими изложенію правилъ ихъ вѣры, принадлежатъ къ вѣроученію, предписывающему своимъ послѣдователямъ подчиняться какъ верховной власти той страны, въ которой они проживаютъ, такъ и существующему въ ней порядку, Министерство отъ 14 чис. Января № сообщило Ковенскому Губернатору, что, въ виду ВЫСОЧАЙШАГО Манифеста 17 Октября 1905 года, оно не встрѣчаетъ препятствій къ допущенію устройства послѣдователями сей секты молитвенныхъ собраній въ названномъ селеніи, съ возложеніемъ на полицію лишь обязанности наблюденія за тѣмъ, чтобы въ собраніяхъ этихъ сектантовъ не происходило ничего незаконнаго и противнаго нравственности и общественному порядку. Что же касается ходатайства названныхъ лицъ объ устройствѣ молитвеннаго дома и о назначеніи для нихъ особаго проповѣдника, то ходатайство сіе можетъ быть удовлетворено не ранѣе изданія въ законодательномъ порядкѣ правилъ, опредѣляющихъ порядокъ образованія и способъ дѣятельности принадлежащихъ къ христіанскимъ вѣроученіямъ различныхъ общинъ, непредусмотрѣнныхъ дѣйствующими узаконеніями. Въ настоящее время въ Департаментѣ Духовныхъ Дѣлъ Иностранныхъ Исповѣданій приступлено уже къ составленію таковыхъ правилъ, причемъ будетъ принято во вниманіе и изложенное выше ходатайство просителей объ упорядоченіи веденія ихъ метрическихъ записей.

Директоръ

Начальникъ Отдѣленія

МИНИСТЕРСТВО ВНУТРЕННИХЪ ДѢЛЪ.

ДЕПАРТАМЕНТЪ ДУХОВНЫХЪ ДѢЛЪ иностранныхъ исповѣданій.

12 Апрѣля 1906 г.

№ 639

Въ Канцелярію Виленскаго, Ковенскаго и Гродненскаго Генералъ-Губернатора.

Виленскій, Ковенскій и Гродненскій Генералъ-Губернаторъ, отъ 28 мин. Января, № 636, сообщилъ Министерству ходатайство послѣдователей методистскаго ученія, проживающихъ въ с. Шанцахъ, Ковенскаго уѣзда, о разрѣшеніи имъ отправлять богослуженіе по обрядамъ ихъ вѣры и о дозволеніи имъ устроить въ этомъ селеніи молитвенный домъ, съ особымъ проповѣдникомъ при ономъ.

Изъ дѣлъ Департамента усматривается, что съ приведеннымъ ходатайствомъ названные просители обращались непосредственно въ Министерство Внутреннихъ Дѣлъ въ Октябрѣ прошлаго 1905 г., причемъ просили также о возложеніи на проповѣдника ихъ общины обязанности веденія метрическихъ книгъ для членовъ оной. По разсмотрѣніи сего ходатайства Министерство нашло, что исповѣданіе методистской секты не признано въ установленномъ порядкѣ въ предѣлахъ Имперіи, и что по сему вопросъ о допущеніи въ настоящее время дѣятельности этой секты на одинаковыхъ основаніяхъ съ признанными въ Россіи иновѣрными исповѣданіями, само собою разумѣется, подлежитъ разрѣшенію въ отрицательномъ смыслѣ. Но принявъ во вниманіе, что, на основаніи ст. 45 Осн. Гос. Зак., свобода вѣры присвояется не только христіанамъ иностран-

на благоусмотрѣніе Вашего Высокопревосходительства, потому, что так как ни въ образѣ жизни методистовъ, ни въ ученіи ихъ не заключается ничего предосудительнаго, то я съ своей стороны не встрѣчалъ бы препятствій къ удовлетворенію ихъ просьбы.-

При семъ прилагаются: списокъ послѣдователей секты методистовъ и основныя правила ихъ вѣры.-

И. д. Губернатора *[подпись]*

Вице Губернатора *[подпись]*

И. д. Совѣтника *[подпись]*

Секретарь *[подпись]*

Not long after the birth of the MEC in Kaunas a congregation was established in Kybartai/Virbalis, Lithuania, adjacent to the German border of East Prussia. Along with Kaunas, it remained part of the annual conference of Northern Germany until 1907. On February 7, 1909, a church building was dedicated by Bishop William Burt in Kybartai/Virbalis. This was the first MEC building erected on the soil of the Russian Empire.

The following year a beautiful church was constructed in Kaunas and dedicated on January 14, 1911, by Bishop William Burt, who made the following comments about that occasion.

Methodist Episcopal Church, Kybartai

Saturday, Jan. 14th, was a beautiful winter day, cold and crisp, with a bright sun and blue sky. There was enough snow for good sleighing, and sleighs of many varieties were rushing to and fro.

The children also were enjoying a winter holiday. The whole scene was characteristically Russian, and the sleigh bells made merry music.

Methodist Episcopal Church, Kaunas, Lithuania, known as the "Mother Church of Russian Methodism"

Interior of the Methodist Episcopal Church, Kaunas, Lithuania

When at 11 a.m. we entered the Church for the dedication service, 550 people were there awaiting us. Of course, Dr. G. A. Simons was there and served as interpreter. Five of our German ministers came over to assist in the services. The musical program prepared and directed by Mrs. Durdis was excellent, and the whole service made a profound impression on all present.

From 6 to 9 in the evening there was an interesting song service interspersed with several brief addresses. At this service by actual count 700 people were packed into the Church, and to our great surprise and delight His Excellency General Werrewkin, the Governor of the Province, and his charming wife were present. He is a superb looking man with a very intelligent and kind face. The wife is of English origin and said that her grandfather's name was Ellis. She seemed much pleased to hear the English language spoken. The Governor made a neat little address in Russian and we greeted each other in German. Since this is one of the most important provinces in Russia, it meant much for our Church at Kowno [Kaunas] and for all our work in Russia to have such a man present on this historic occasion. We were much encouraged by these two tokens of royal favor, namely, the voluntary and hearty permission of the Czar, and the presence of the Governor and his wife."[1]

The year 1907 was extremely important year the emergence of Methodism in Russia. Because of the efforts of Bishop William Burt, the Methodist Episcopal leader in charge of Europe, the General Missionary Committee appropriated $1,000 for work in Russia. In the spring of that year Bishop Burt appointed the Rev. Hjalmar Salmi, who was born in St. Petersburg, as pastor there. He was fluent in Finnish, Swedish, and Russian, had studied theology in Helsinki, Finland, and had some pastoral experience among Finnish Americans. On March 2, 1907, he received permission to preach in St. Petersburg, providing he avoided political subjects and worked also in Finnish-Russian villages. In and around St. Petersburg there were sizable Swedish and Finnish populations; hence, ministries were begun in three languages: Russian, Swedish, and Finnish.

---

[1] William Burt, "A Memorable Day in Kowno [Kaunas], Russia," *Methodism in Europe*, Volume IV, No. 2 (June 1911): 3–4.

The Rev. Hjalmar Salmi

The following document, dated March 2, 1907, from the Governor of St. Petersburg is of historic importance, for it granted the Rev. Salmi the right to hold Methodist services in that city. Salmi was a person of unusual gifts and indeed possessed the qualities and skills needed for the development of Methodist Episcopal outreach in Russia. He was born and educated in St. Petersburg, which gave him many advantages, for he knew the language, the culture, and the people.

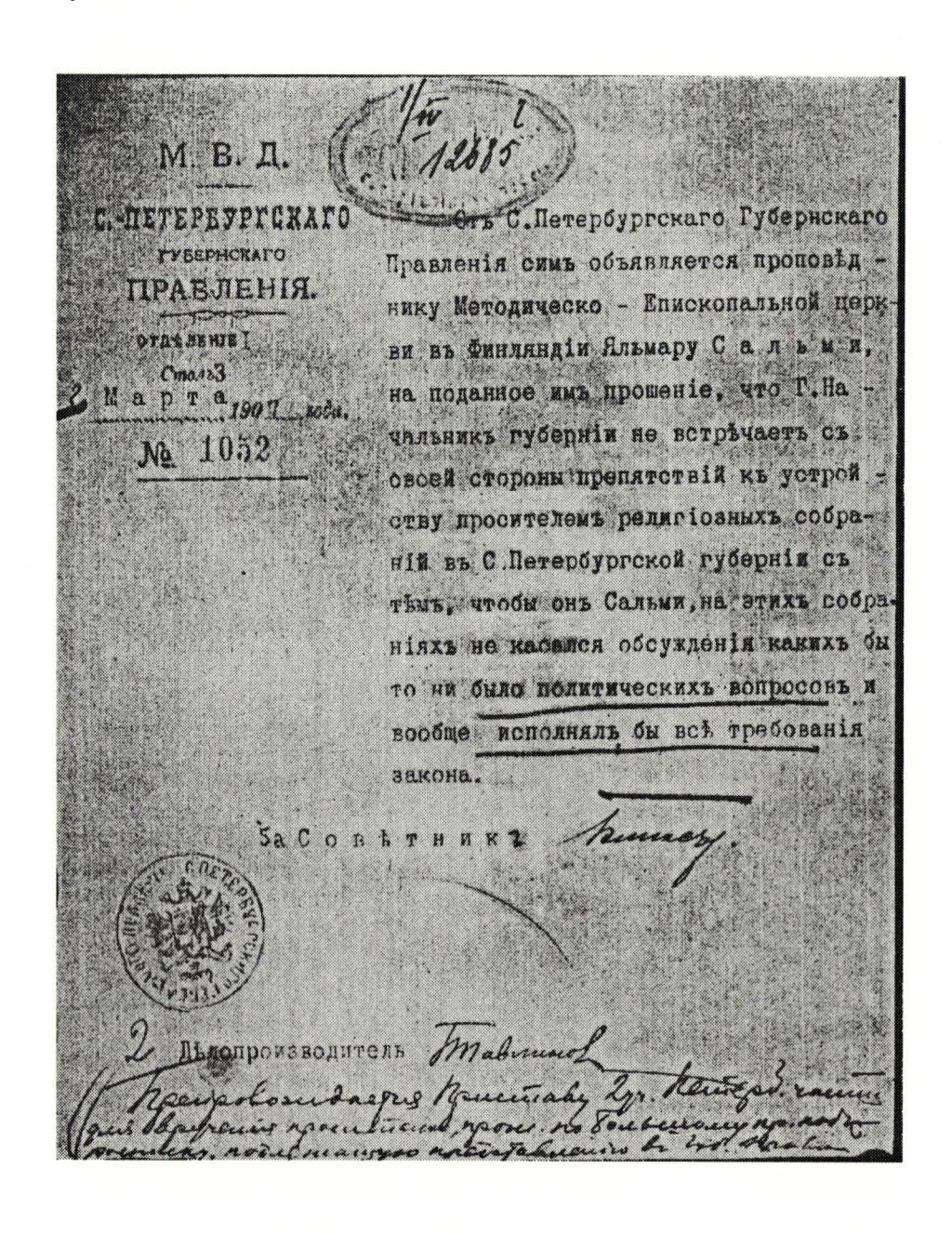

Freely translated, the document reads:

> The administration of the St. Petersburg Government hereby informs the preacher, Hjalmar Salmi, of the Methodist Episcopal Church in Finland, that the Governor of the Government does not object on his part, to the holding of meetings by the petitioner in the Government of St. Petersburg, on condition that he, Salmi, must not discuss *political questions* in these meetings, and in general must *fulfill all demands of the law.*[2]

In the fall of 1907, Bishop Burt appointed the American, the Rev. George A. Simons (1874–1952) of the New York East Annual Conference, as superintendent of the Russian Mission. On October 10, 1907, he arrived in St. Petersburg and began work with his assistants, lay preacher K. U. Strandross and Salmi. Regular worship services were inaugurated on November 3, 1907.

Simons, who soon became fluent in the Russian language, related a fascinating story of the first sermon he preached in Russia, for which Salmi served as his translator.

The Rev. George A. Simons

> Accepting the urgent invitation of my enthusiastic assistant, the Rev. Hjalmar Salmi, to preach to our congregation at Handrovo, a village about two hours' travel by train from St. Petersburg, a service was arranged for Saturday evening, October 12, 1907, my third day in Russia. It was in a peasant's dwelling where the meeting was held. The room was crowded with more than one hundred and fifty persons, nearly all of whom were standing, eagerly listening to the gospel message. They were closely packed together like sardines in a tin box. My subject was, "How to enter the kingdom of God." My text was Mark 10:15—"Verily I say unto you, Whosoever shall not receive the kingdom of God as a little child, he shall in no wise enter therein." I never had a better time preaching. Brother Salmi acted as my interpreter. Having been born and educated in St. Petersburg, he was a linguist of considerable ability. He could preach in at least four languages.
>
> Two small windows were open, and a score or more folks gathered around them to hear the sermon. When the writer had finished speaking and Brother Salmi had concluded with a fervent prayer, there rushed into the room an infuriated man, flashing a long knife and commanding us all to leave the house immediately. He was evidently under the influence of vodka, Russian whisky. With superhuman strength of an intoxicated man he wedged his way through the crowd. He tried to get at the pastor and myself, who were standing behind a small table in the corner, and when he was only a few feet away from us, Brother Salmi advised me to jump out of the window, and thus make my escape. Alas, the window seemed less than three feet square, and I had my doubts about getting through it. I remember saying that "necessity is the mother of invention." Indeed one never knows how seemingly impossible things become really possible until an exigency arises that demands fearless and speedy action. Thus spurred on by a keen sense of the imminent situation, I doubled myself up as expeditiously as I could, plunged out into the Egyptian darkness, fortunately landing on my feet, with the pastor tumbling after. Brother Salmi hastily led me to a cow-barn next door, and there we hid for a

---

[2] "Report of Dr. G. A. Simons," *Minutes of the Finland and St. Petersburg Mission Conference of The Methodist Episcopal Church, Fifth Session, August 26–20, 1908* (Rome: Methodist Press, 1908), p. 29.

House in the village of Handrovo where Simons preached his first sermon

few minutes until some of our friends had led the disturber away.

We went into the house where we were to be "entertained" for the night, our would-be slayer and a few of his comrades still threatening to catch us. . . .

The only bed in the house was assigned to the writer. . . . As I lay there, unable to sleep, I did some good hard thinking and earnest praying. I promised the Lord that if He would get me out of that place and back to my Hotel in St. Petersburg in safety the next morning, some day I would build a chapel in that village. . . .

Before closing this chapter may I say that the promise which I made to God that night in the peasant's home was really kept. In the summer of 1913, we built a chapel with a parsonage and a children's home all under one roof. The building was dedicated by the late Bishop Wilson S. Lewis, LL.D., who was then one of the Methodist bishops for China, and he was assisted by the late Dr. John F. Goucher, founder of Goucher College in Baltimore, and the late Dr. George Heber Jones, who was one of the pioneer Methodist missionaries in Korea. The children's home was named for our sainted mother, who had spent only a brief year with us and was buried in the Protestant Cemetery in St. Petersburg.

Many a time we tried to persuade the man who tried to take our life to make us a present of the long

Sister Anna, women, and children at the Ottilie Simons Children's Home, Handrovo

knife as a memento of the historic occasion, but he would not comply with our request. He wished to have the unhappy incident blotted out. He had become one of our best friends and assured us again and again that it was not he but the cursed vodka that was responsible for doing the thing that he so much regretted."[3]

In Estonia and Latvia, which were also a part of Tsarist Russia, Methodism was also born in the early 1900s. In 1907, Vassili Täht, a native-born Estonian from the village of Leisi and a colporteur of the British Bible Society, who, according to George A. Simons' "Report of the Superintendent" (1910), had become an "evangelist-at-large" for the MEC in the Baltics, and Karl Kuum, an Estonian farmer and Moravian lay preacher, arrived on the island of Sareemaa and began to preach the gospel in Kuressaare.

After much success in evangelization, they met in 1908 to commemorate the death of Christ in an apartment in Kurressaare. This was the actual beginning of the first MEC congregation in Estonia, though it was not formally established until August 12, 1910, when George A. Simons and Vassili Täht received three men and three women into membership of the MEC in Estonia.

Vassili Täht

Karl Kuum

At the Finnish Annual Conference of 1910, Vassili Täht was assigned as pastor to Kuressaare, and in 1912 a church was built there. Martin Prikask, an Estonian who was converted in one of the evangelizations in Kuressaare, was later appointed as a lay preacher in Kuressaare and began successful evangelizations in more rural areas.

In 1910 Riga, Latvia, also became a Methodist appointment. The following year the Rev. Georg Durdis, who had been assigned by the Northern German Annual Conference in 1907 to serve as the minister in Kaunas, was transferred to Riga and Latvia became a part of the Finland and Russia Mission Conference.

Of equal importance was the mission work in Latvia of the *Evangelische Gemeinschaft* (The Evangelical Church), which later united with the Church of the United Brethren in Christ to form the Evangelical United Brethren Church, which subsequently joined with The Methodist Church in 1968 to form The United Methodist Church. At the annual meeting of the Board of Missions of The Evangelical Church in the United States in October 1910, the decision was made officially to start mission work in Latvia, and the Woman's Missionary Society agreed to pay the salary of a missionary. The work of both The Evangelical Church and the MEC in Latvia grew effectively and established a significant number of congregations

Martin Prikask

---

[3] George A. Simons, "Observations and Experiences in Russia and the Baltic Countries," *The European Harvest Field*, published monthly by the American-European Fellowship for Christian Oneness and Evangelization (New York, October 1929), Volume X, No. 10, pp. 17–19.

throughout the country from 1910 to 1940. Though some of the early work was done in the German language, in both churches it moved rather swiftly into the indigenous Latvian language. Of course, many people spoke Russian, which also made communication possible throughout the early mission work of Methodists in the countries located within Tsarist Russia. In Riga the Bethany ME Church was built specifically for Russian-language ministries. See the photograph of the church building on page 36.

St. Petersburg and Surrounding Area

The primary locus of MEC mission within Russia proper was first and foremost in and around St. Petersburg. The early efforts of evangelization by Swedish Methodists have already been discussed, as well as the official beginning of the MEC Mission in St. Petersburg with the assignment of Salmi and Simons. The work was further enhanced in 1908, when Bishop William Burt appointed Finnish-born deaconess Anna Eklund to St. Petersburg. She had been educated at the Bethany Deaconess Training Center in Hamburg, Germany, as well as at the Training Center in Frankfurt, Germany, and was consecrated as a deaconess in 1886, at the annual meeting of the Finland and Russia Mission Conference. The only money available to fund her work in Russia was a donation of $100 by Bishop William Burt.

Even so, soon this energetic woman had enlisted five dedicated young women, and a Bethany Deaconess Home was opened in St. Petersburg. She was a faithful champion of the poor and hungry, seeking support from every possible quarter. She procured bread from local bakers, food and clothing from the wealthy, and worked in government hospitals and orphanages. The children's home in the village of Handrovo has already been mentioned. It is difficult to communicate the swiftness with which Sister Anna moved the deaconess work forward, but it is one of the amazing stories in the history of the deaconess movement.

Simons, Salmi, and Eklund formed a most effective leadership team for the MEC in Russia. Sister Anna energetically and effectively developed the deaconess work.[4] Though it was strongly humanitarian, Simons encouraged her and one of her coworkers, Sister Ada, to preach in the neighboring villages of Haitolovo and Sigolovo, where MEC chapels were soon built.

Sister Anna modeled selfless deaconess service in many ways. She had no reservations whatsoever about ministering to the sick and wounded in the Red Army hospitals of St. Petersburg. Where there was human need, she was ready to serve. When it came to the distribution of clothing and food for the hungry, there were no political, economic, or religious prerequisites.

Sister Anna Eklund

---

[4] For more information about this amazing woman, see this author's book *Sister Anna Eklund (1867–1949): A Methodist Saint in Russia* (New York: GBGM Books, 2001).

Left: *Sister Ada [standing] and Sister Natalie [seated], recruited by Sister Anna, are pictured with children of the Ottilie Simons Children's Home in Handrovo, Russia.*

Methodist Episcopal Chapel and Parsonage in Haitolovo, Russia

Publications

George A. Simons and Hjalmar Salmi were strong advocates of the Wesleyan tradition and began an intensive publication program of translations of Wesleyan literature and new materials. In January 1908, Simons initiated an English-language quarterly newsletter, *Methodism in Russia*. Published at the Methodist Publishing House in Rome, its purpose was to tell the story of the MEC's mission in Finland and Russia. On page 1 of the first issue one reads, "This Quarterly is sent *free of charge* to friends in America and Europe who are willing to pray daily for evangelization of Russia." Information was also provided as to how those who wished to support the mission financially might contribute. "Churches and Missions" are listed without distinction. Nineteen are listed for Finland and the following for Russia: Handrovo Circuit (Sigolovo, Uusikyla, Markovo, Haitala, and Metsäpirtti), pastor, the Rev. Hjalmar Salmi;

Kowno [Kaunas] Circuit (Kaunas, Vilnius, and Kybartai/Virbalis), pastor, the Rev. Georg R. Durdis; St. Petersburg (Finnish, Swedish, and Russian ministries), pastors, the Rev. Hjalmar Salmi and local preacher, K. U. Strandroos. Below is a reprint of the title page of the first issue.

Methodism in Russia

A QUARTERLY PUBLISHED IN THE INTEREST
OF THE METHODIST EPISCOPAL CHURCH IN FINLAND AND RUSSIA

Volume I   St. Petersburg, January-March, 1908   **No. 1**

THE REV. BISHOP WILLIAM BURT, D.D.
GENERAL SUPERINTENDENT OF THE METHODIST EPISCOPAL CHURCH
RESIDENT IN EUROPE

In 1909 the *Khristianski Pobornik (Christian Advocate)* was launched as a Russian-language publication.[5] The first monthly issue appeared in January 1909 and consisted of eight pages. It was edited by Hjalmar Salmi and reflected a Wesleyan tone from the outset by including on the first page a Russian translation of Charles Wesley's hymn "Jesus, Lover of my soul." While the content was primarily instructional, the magazine was and is an excellent source of knowledge for St. Petersburg Methodism, the daily life of the members and workers, worship life and beliefs, humanitarian outreach, as well as the development of strategy and relations with the authorities, as things became increasingly difficult after the Bolshevik Revolution. The magazine continued in publication in St. Petersburg until the end of 1917. Fortunately an almost complete set of the issues published in St. Petersburg is located in the rare book collection of the St. Petersburg Public Library. After Simons was recalled in 1918 and reassigned to Riga, Latvia, the *Khristianski Pobornik* was revived and published there in Russian.

Though the magazine had five editors in the course of its life (1909–1917), clearly Simons and Salmi played a significant role in the inclusion of Wesleyan theology and history, for which resources in the Russian language were almost non-existent.[6] It would appear that Simons and Salmi had in mind publishing the *Standard Sermons* of John Wesley in Russian. The first four sermons were published consecutively as in *Standard Sermons*. The third of these, however, as indicated below was by Charles Wesley.

1. "Salvation by Faith" (John Wesley, June 11, 1738), Eph. 2:28, *Khristianski Pobornik* 1/2 (February 1909), 9–11, 14–16
2. "The Almost Christian" (John Wesley, July 25, 1741), Acts 26:28, *Khristianski Pobornik* 1/4 (April 1909), 25–27, 32
3. "Awake, Thou That Sleepest" (Charles Wesley, April 4, 1742), Eph. 5:14, *Khristianski Pobornik* 1/5 (May 1909), 33–35, 47–48
4. "Scriptural Christianity" (John Wesley, August 24, 1744), Jn. 4:31, *Khristianski Pobornik* 1/7 (July 1909), 49–51, (August 1909) 57–58, 63
5. "Justification by Faith" (John Wesley, 1746), Rom. 4:5, *Khristianski Pobornik* 1/14 (February 1910), 9–11; 1/15 (March 1910), 17–19, 22–23
6. "The New Birth" (John Wesley, 1760), Jn. 3:7, *Khristianski Pobornik* 1/16 (April 1910), 38-39; 1/18 (June 1910), 45–47

How widely distributed was the periodical, *Khristianski Pobornik*? While this cannot be determined, it is well known that 1,000 copies of each issue were printed.

One other sermon by John Wesley was published as a monograph of *Khristianski Pobornik*, namely, "The Spirit of Bondage and of Adoption" (John Wesley, 1746). A copy of the cover page of the monograph appears on the next page.[7]

---

[5] For more detailed information on the magazine see John Dunstan, "George A. Simons and the *Khristianski Pobornik*," *Methodist History* 19:1 (1980): 21–40.

[6] Interestingly, an Orthodox church history scholar, A. Bulgakov of the Spiritual Academy of the Russian Othodox Church in Kiev, published a two-volume work, *The History of Methodism*, in 1887, which was later used for Russian-language teaching of Methodist history at the MEC Theological Training Institute established in Riga, Latvia.

[7] Note the error in John Wesley's death year. It should be 1791, not 1719. This author has published the seven sermons of the Wesleys as listed above (including the monograph) in an updated Russian edition, *Sermons of John and Charles Wesley* (New York: General Board of Global Ministries, 1995).

Khristianski Pobornik Monograph, John Wesley's Sermon:
"The Spirit of Bondage and Adoption"

ИЗДАНІЕ ХРИСТІАНСКАГО ПОБОРНИКА

ДУХЪ РАБСТВА и ДУХЪ УСЫНОВЛЕНІЯ

ПРОПОВѢДЬ ДЖОНА ВЕСЛИ

ДЖОНЪ ВЕСЛИ
Основатель методизма (1703—1719).

On the following page is an example of a title page of the *Khristianski Pobornik* from March 1910 with a photograph of Bishop William Burt and his wife.

„МІРЪ МОЙ ПРИХОДЪ, А СПАСАТЬ ДУШИ МОЕ ПРИЗВАНІЕ" — Джонъ Веслей

Христіанскій Поборникъ

Русскій органъ Методистской Епископской Церкви

Томъ I-ый, № 15   МАРТЪ 1910   2-й г. изд. № 3

БЕСѢДЫ ДЖОНА ВЕСЛЕЙ

V

Оправданіе вѣрою
(Окончаніе).

II. 1. Но что значитъ быть оправданнымъ и что такое оправданіе? Этотъ вопросъ я и хотѣлъ изъяснить вторымъ. Изъ сказаннаго уже выясняется, что это не значитъ что человѣкъ сдѣлается дѣйствительно правдивымъ и праведнымъ. Это было бы освященіе, которое конечно является однимъ изъ первыхъ плодовъ оправданія, но оно, независимо отъ этаго, есть особенный даръ Божій и, при томъ, совершенно другого характера. Первое состоитъ въ томъ, что Богъ сдѣлалъ *для насъ* чрезъ Сына Своего. Второе же есть то, что Онъ творитъ *въ насъ* чрезъ Духа Святаго, такъ что, хотя въ нѣкоторыхъ рѣдкихъ случаяхъ выраженіе „оправданіе" употребляется въ столь широкомъ смыслѣ, что заключаетъ въ себѣ и понятіе освященія, все же въ обычномъ своемъ значеніи эти слова явно отличаются одно отъ другого, въ посланіяхъ какъ ап. Павла, такъ и прочихъ вдохновенныхъ писателей.

2. Нельзя подтвердить яснымъ текстомъ Священнаго Писанія, того широко распространеннаго понятія, чтобы оправданіе освободило насъ отъ обвиненія, въ особенности отъ клеветы сатаны. Во всемъ матеріалѣ Св. Писанія, касающемся этого вопроса, не встрѣчается ни слова о клеветникѣ или о его клеветѣ, хотя въ сущности нельзя отрицать, что сатана является нашимъ клеветникомъ, ибо его ясно называ-

Епископъ Буртъ и его супруга

ютъ таиъ (Откр. 12:10). Но великій апостолъ ни въ одномъ мѣстѣ своихъ посланій, говорящихъ объ оправданіи, ни къ Римлянамъ, ни къ Галатамъ, не указываетъ на это.

Также легче предполагать, чѣмъ доказать какимъ-нибудь яснымъ текстомъ изъ Писанія, что оправданіе освобождаетъ насъ отъ обвиненія провозглашеннаго противъ насъ закономъ. Во всякомъ случаѣ, чтобы объяснить этотъ необычайный образъ выраженія, я этимъ хочу сказать ни болѣе ни менѣе, что хотя мы согрѣшили противъ закона Божія, и этимъ заслужили гибель въ аду, Богъ не приводитъ въ исполненіе надъ тѣми, которые оправданы, *вполнѣ заслуженнаго* ими наказанія.

4. Меньше всего оправданіе означаетъ, чтобы Богъ поддался обману относительно тѣхъ, которыхъ Онъ оправдываетъ, чтобы Онъ считалъ ихъ такими, какими они не являются въ дѣйствительности и признавалъ ихъ иными, чѣмъ они есть. Оно ни въ какомъ случаѣ не означаетъ, чтобы Богъ судилъ о насъ противно истинному положенію дѣла, чтобы Онъ оцѣнилъ больше, чѣмъ въ дѣйствительности стоимъ или предполагалъ, что мы праведны, тогда какъ мы нечестивы. Воистину, не такъ. Оцѣнка Премудраго Бога всегда согласна съ истиной. Также не можетъ согласоваться съ никогда не заблуждающейся премудростью, считать меня невиннымъ, принимать меня за праведнаго и святого лишь потому, что другой святъ. Въ этомъ отношеніи Богъ не можетъ смѣшивать меня со Христомъ, какъ и не съ Давидомъ или Авраамомъ. Пусть каждый, кому Богъ далъ разумъ, взвѣситъ это безъ предубѣжденія

A number of other publications appeared in the *Khristianski Pobornik* series, such as the booklet, *Who Are the Methodists and What Do They Want?* (See its cover at left.) This twenty-four-page booklet discussed the origins of Methodism, its basic beliefs, its worldwide breadth, and its contemporary significance. Other publications included: a Russian translation of John Wesley's *Character of a Methodist,* a large portion of *Doctrines and Discipline of the Methodist Episcopal Church,* Russian translations of Bishop William Burt's *Handbook for Probationers,* and his book *Homiletics.*

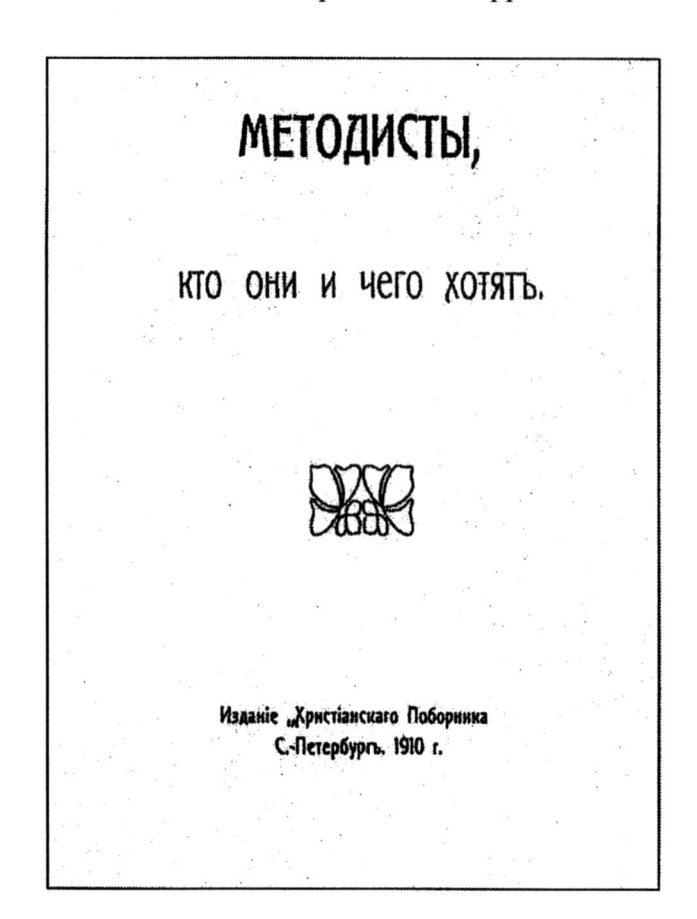

One cannot overemphasize the diligence of George A. Simons and Hjalmar Salmi in developing appropriate literature for the work of the MEC in Russia and the Baltic States.

Simons published a hymnbook in 1913, which consisted of some 100 western hymns translated into Russian. He also published a *Methodist Episcopal Catechism* for use with all those interested in the beliefs of Methodist Episcopal Christians and in becoming members of the MEC.

Registration

The year 1909 was pivotal for Methodism in Russia proper, for this was the year in which Dr. George A. Simons succeeded in the legal registration of the MEC in St. Petersburg. The date of the official registration was June 12, 1909, according to the letter of Mr. V. Smirnov, Vice-Director of the Department of Spiritual Affairs of Foreign Confessions of the Ministry of Home Affairs, dated January 6, 1910, and directed to the governor of St. Petersburg. The letter raises the question as to whether the registration conforms to the stipulation of the Imperial ordinance of October 1906, which stated that the establishment of such congregations can be only for those persons who have left the Orthodox Church.

A second letter dated February 12, 1910, to the Department of Spiritual Affairs of Foreign Confessions directed to the governor of St. Petersburg confirmed that the members of the First Methodist Episcopal Church in St. Petersburg[8] consisted not only of persons of foreign confessions but also those who have left the Orthodox Church. English translations precede both copies of the original Russian-language letters.

---

[8] Though this was the officially registered name, the name used was ME Church of Christ Our Savior.

Letter 1

Ministry of Home Affairs[9]
Department of Spiritual Affairs of Foreign Confessions
St. Petersburg

January 8, 1910

To: The Governor of St. Petersburg

According to the decree of the Government of St. Petersburg Province of June 12, 1909, a religious congregation was registered under the name of "The First Methodist Episcopal Church in Saint Petersburg."

Taking into account the fact that the Imperial ordinance of October 17, 1906, stipulates the establishment of congregations only for those persons who have left Orthodoxy, the Department of Spiritual Affairs humbly requests your Excellency to notify if this circumstance was borne in mind when registering this congregation.

Vice-Director (signed): V. Smirnov
Official of a Special Commission (with seal): Pavlov
Certified to be true.

Letter 2

Ministry of Home Affairs
Governor of St. Petersburg
for St. Petersburg Province

February 12, 1910

To: The Department of Spiritual Affairs of Foreign Confessions

I would like to notify the Department that the congregation called "The First Methodist Episcopal Church in Saint Petersburg" was registered after making inquiries at the Department about the possibility of such registration and in view of the fact that its members comprised not only people of foreign confessions but also those who had left Orthodoxy.

Governor
Counselor

---

[9] This author was fortunate to receive copies of both of these letters from the National Archives in St. Petersburg in 1995, while doing research for the volume *Methodism in Russia and the Baltic States: History and Renewal*.

Letter 1

М. В. Д.
Департаментъ
Духовныхъ Дѣлъ
Иностранныхъ Исповѣданій.
8 Января 1910 г.
№ 252

С.-Петербургскому Губернатору.

Журнальнымъ постановленіемъ С.-Петербургскаго Губернскаго Правленія 12-го іюня мин. года зарегистрирована религіозная община подъ названіемъ "Первая Методистская Епископская церковь въ С.-Петербургѣ."

Принимая во вниманіе, что ВЫСОЧАЙШИМЪ Указомъ 17 октября 1906 г. предусмотрѣно образованіе общинъ лишь для сектантовъ, отпавшихъ отъ Православія, Департаментъ Духовныхъ Дѣлъ покорнѣйше проситъ Ваше Превосходительство не отказать въ увѣдомленіи имѣлось ли въ виду это обстоятельство при регистраціи общины.

Вице-Директоръ (подписалъ) В. Смирновъ.
Чиновникъ Особыхъ Порученій (скрѣпилъ) Павловъ.
Вѣрно:

Letter 2

М. В. Д.

С.-ПЕТЕРБУРГСКІЙ
ГУБЕРНАТОРЪ.
по
ГУБЕРНСКОМУ ПРАВЛЕНІЮ.

Столъ 3

12 февраля 1910 г.

№ 104

Губернаторъ

Въ Департаментъ Духовныхъ Дѣлъ
Иностранныхъ Исповѣданій.-

1736

Увѣдомляю Департаментъ, что религіозная Община подъ названіемъ "Первая Методистская Епископская церковь въ С.Петербургѣ" была зарегистрирована послѣ наведенной въ Департаментѣ справки о возможности такой регистраціи и въ виду наличности въ числѣ ея членовъ помимо лицъ инославныхъ исповѣданій, и лицъ, отпавшихъ отъ православія.

Совѣтникъ

The Methodist Episcopal Church Russia Mission Grows

From its beginning in 1907 until 1911, the MEC's work in Russia came under the Finland and Russian Mission and the episcopal supervision of Bishop William Burt (1852–1936). Burt was born in Padstow of Cornwall in England and did his university studies in the United States. In 1881 he became a member of the New York East Annual Conference of the MEC. After his election as bishop, he was assigned to Central and Eastern Europe and moved to Zürich, Switzerland. Bishop Burt was responsible for having organized the MEC Russia Mission. In 1911, the work in St. Petersburg was organized as its own mission, the Russia Mission Conference. The Finland and St. Petersburg Mission had originally been established in 1892 by Bishop Isaac Wilson Joyce.

Rarely mentioned in the story of early Russian Methodism is the Russian-Swedish work in Viborg and Russian outreach in Helsinki with a population of some 25,000 Russians. In the 1910 *Annual Report of the Board of Foreign Missions of the Methodist Episcopal Church* the Rev. N. J. Rosen submitted this report regarding Viborg:

> The Russian work has been carried on side by side with the Swedish. I have had no one to help me, with the exception of one visit from Brother Salmi. My regular interpreter, Mrs. Helenius, has not been able to come all the time, and so I have spoken in English, with Mrs. Schroeder as interpreter. Russian services have been held twice every week besides extra meetings on holidays. . . . I am glad to acknowledge the good proofs of a changed life among our Russian members. Genuine Christian love and peace mark all their dealings. So as not to burden our Russian friends financially, we did not ask them to contribute toward our current expenses. But with tears they came and begged for the privilege of participating with their Swedish brethren in bearing the financial burdens. Since then they have helped raise the pastor's salary and other expenses. During the year I have visited regularly every month Rokkala and Kirkoniemi, about thirty kilometers east of Viborg, where there are two large glass factories with hundreds of workmen of various nationalities, especially Swedes and Russians. Our Russian exhorter, Brother Miranoff, has also visited these places and preached to his countrymen. Some have been converted, and last time we spoke of organizing a class there. The great need of our Viborg society is a church for the Swedes and Russians, or at least a more convenient hall for our meetings.[10]

The following year the Board of Foreign Missions provided funding for the rental of a large hall in the heart of the city for worship services and other activities of the Russian-Swedish work. In addition to the outreach ministries already being pursued, in June of 1911, the Rev. Rosen reported that work was begun in the harbor, visited every year by about 2,000 vessels, among the seamen.

The MEC seminary in Helsinki was also important at this time in educating persons for ministry with knowledge of the Russian language.

Once the Russia Mission was separated from the Finnish Conference, however, one reads little more in the official reports of the Board of Foreign Missions about the Russian-Swedish or Russian-Finnish work outside Russia proper.

Superintendent Simons' reports for the years 1910 and 1911 give one an indication of the extent of the activity and effectiveness of the MEC Mission in Russia. The 1910 report is divided primarily into two parts: "The Work on the Finnish District" and "The Work on the Rus-

---

[10] *Annual Report of the Board of Foreign Missions of the Methodist Episcopal Church* (New York: Board of Foreign Missions, 1910), pp. 478–79.

sian District." The latter included Russia proper (St. Petersburg, Sigolovo, and Handrovo), Lithuania (Kaunas and Virbalis/Kybartai), Russian Karelia, Finland (Viborg), Estonia (Kuressaare) and Latvia, and Marinsk (Siberia). In 1910 Simons reported on the number of conversions (500), Epworth Leagues (youth organization), men's groups, Sunday Schools, the extent of the women and children's work, and the amount of local contributions to missions in China and India. Of the work in Marinsk, Simons wrote:

> Last February Brother August Karlson, a Russian-Estonian, for some years a colporteur of the British and Foreign Bible Society, visited St. Petersburg, attended our services, begged to have Methodist literature and the privilege of attending our class. He spent about ten weeks with us and studied our Methodist history, polity, and doctrine quite thoroughly. Since returning to Marinsk, which is about four–days journey from St. Petersburg, he has been organizing Methodist classes in several places. Thus, Methodism has already reached Siberia.[11]

Adalbert Lukas

Simons' reports indicate his deep interest in the training of pastors and workers for Russian-language ministries of the MEC. Here is a brief summary of that part of his 1910 report:

(1) Julius F. Hecker, a native of St. Petersburg, graduated this June with honors from Baldwin–Wallace College. He expects to return to St. Petersburg after his graduation from the theological seminary at Drew University.

(2) Erich von Molitz, a native of Virbalis/Kybartai, was at Northwestern University, Evanston, Illinois, where he has been in charge of a Russian mission in Chicago for the past year.

(3) Karl Adeloff, a native of Vilnius, spent one and a quarter year at the Methodist Theological Institute at Frankfurt-am-Main, Germany, but was called into Russian military service in November. After his two years and eight months of service are completed, he will return to Frankfurt-am-Main to continue his studies.

(4) Rudolf Brennheiser, a native of Kaunas, has completed two years of the four-year course of study at Frankfurt-am-Main. During Simons' absence in Edinburgh, he supplied the pulpit in St. Petersburg and made an evangelistic tour through the Baltic States.

(5) Alfred Hühn of south Russia has spent two years at Frankfurt-am-Main. During the summer he assisted Pastor Durdis in Virbalis/Kybartai and Kaunas.

(6) Paul Ludwig, of Tomaszow, Russian Poland, spent one year at Frankfurt-am-Main and can preach in Russian, Polish, and German.

(7) August Röandt, a Russian Estonian, who taught at an orphan school in Tallinn, will enter Frankfurt-am-Main in the summer.

---

[11] Unpublished "Report of the Superintendent, George Albert Simons, M.A., D.D." (1910), p. 16.

(8) Adalbert Lukas, a native of St. Petersburg, will also go to Frankfurt-am-Main. He was one of George A. Simons' first recruits for ministry but he was drafted into military service. [After returning to St. Petersburg, he became an editor of the *Khristianski Pobornik.*]

(9, 10) Vladimir Datt and Alexander Ivanoff are studying under the tutelage of George A. Simons.

(11) Olga Hecker, also a native of St. Petersburg and sister of Julius F. Hecker, is preparing for Christian education at Baldwin–Wallace College in Berea, Ohio.

(12, 13) Sisters Ada and Natalie were sent as probationary deaconesses for training to the Bethany Deaconess Motherhouse in Frankfurt-am-Main. Sister Ada understands Finnish, Swedish, German, and Russian, and Sister Natalie understands Estonian, Russian, and German. Both have completed eighteen months of training and have received a diploma from the Governor Inspector of Germany.

Simons' correspondence with the Board of Foreign Missions from the time of his move to St. Petersburg indicates his desire and struggle to procure appropriate property for a mission headquarters which would have multiple purposes: missionary residence, place of worship, educational and humanitarian aid activities, etc. There was an interesting succession of property locations before Simons eventually was able to purchase the property at 58, Bolshoi Prospekt.

> 1907 (Nov. 3): The First ME Society began services at No. 15, 10th Line.
>
> 1908: The Society moved from No. 15 to No. 37, 10th Line, a two-storied brickbuilding with attics. It was owned by a Jewish orphans' home.
>
> 1908: Simons lived at No. 24, Gogolya Street.
>
> 1908: Salmi lived at No. 33, Bolshoi Street.
>
> 1908 (Nov. 3): Bethany (*Vifaniya*) Deaconess Home was opened in a five-room apartment No. 10 at 44, 3rd Line. Later it moved to No. 34, 9th Line.
>
> 1909 (June): At the time of legalization of the first MEC of St. Petersburg its location was Wassili Ostroff, No. 37, 10th Line.
>
> 1909: Simons moved to Apartment No. 13, 18th Line.
>
> 1912: The MEC meeting place was moved to No. 3 ulitsa Malaya Grebetskaya on Petrogradskaya Storono Island, northeast of Vasilevski Ostrov. The new location was known as Fyodorova's Hall.

1914: Simons purchased the property at No. 58, Bolshoi Propekt, on the southeast corner of the junction with the 20th Line. On Dec. 20, 1914, Simons received permission to open a house of worship.

Left: *ME Church of Christ Our Savior, 58 Bolshoi Prospekt, St. Petersburg*

Left: *Interior of the ME Church of Christ Our Savior at 58 Bolshoi Prospekt, St. Petersburg*

The ME Church of Christ Our Savior in St. Petersburg was dedicated on Sunday, March 14, 1915. The pulpit and communion table came from the Methodist Boys' Industrial School in Venice, Italy, and were a gift to the first Methodist class in St. Petersburg. The organ was donated by the Ladies' Aid Society. The statue of the Risen Christ by Thorwaldsen, used quite extensively in the Methodist churches of the Scandinavian countries, was also a gift. The communion service came from one of Simons' friends in the United States.

The best description of the MEC building appears in Bishop John L. Nuelsen's 1923 "Report on Russia to the Executive Committee of the Board of Foreign Missions of the Methodist Episcopal Church":

> Our headquarters are located on the Vassili Island, a section of the city mostly inhabited by the better classes of foreigners. I found the church property in good order. It consists of a two-story frame house with ample space in front and some buildings in the rear, formerly used as a barn and stable. The house was formerly a private residence. By taking away the partitions, a commodious auditorium was secured seating about 300 persons. Besides there are rooms for study classes, library, and a sleeping room occupied by two young girls, candidates for Deaconess work. On the upper floor are the apartments of Dr. Simons, of Sister Anna, of the present Pastor, Bro. Pöld, an office, and two large rooms used for social purposes. Poor people and children are received in these rooms; meals and clothing are distributed, and a beginning was made to give sewing lessons to young girls. I found the rooms in good order. Nothing had been stolen, nothing commandeered by the government. The appearance of the property outside and within is in decided contrast to the conditions prevailing in Petrograd today. When the property was purchased, it was deemed best to have it entered upon the records as the property of Dr. Geo. A. Simons, the Board of Foreign Missions not having a legal status in Russia. Like all other property ours has been nationalized. Technically the State owns all properties, but the former owners are permitted to occupy their property on condition that they keep it in repair and pay an annual tax. The churches are exempt from the tax but must pay "insurance" which is quite high. As a matter of fact, it is equivalent to a tax. Thus far we have not been disturbed in any way. The property is in need of repairs. A good fence was built from lumber of the relief boxes. The fence has been painted and is in good condition. The house needs a new coat of paint; the plumbing needs repair and also the roof. For all these years no repairs have been made. The architect, as well as other experts whom I consulted, state that unless these repairs and

painting can be done before winter the house will greatly suffer. The estimated cost is $1,000. I ordered the repairs and advanced the money from relief funds.[12]

While the MEC work in Russia proper was centered in and around St. Petersburg, it was by no means limited to that area. The outreach in the Baltic States has already been emphasized, and we shall return to it later. The annual reports of Simons in 1910 and 1911 mention the mission initiative undertaken in Marinsk, Siberia, by August Karlson, a Russian-Estonian and MEC evangelist. After his arrival in 1910, Karlson began preaching and organizing classes in Marinsk and neighboring villages. Four years later he was working in seven different villages.[13] In 1914, as a result of his work, a MEC chapel was built in Vambolsk. In December of that year Martin Prikask traveled for nine days to reach Vambolsk in order to dedicate the building at its official opening.

The Annual Session of Preachers and Helpers of the MEC in Russia, held in St. Petersburg, August 1916
Seated left to right: Sister Anna Eklund, Oskar Pöld, George A. Simons, Martin Prikask, Sister Ada
Standing: center is Miss Ottilie Simons (George A. Simons' sister), to her right is Karl Kuum

The work of the MEC in Russia indeed thrived during the tenure of Simons as superintendent, especially until the time of the Bolshevik Revolution. As already noted, students were studying to be Russian-language pastors and deaconesses. Congregations were growing and new ones being established. Compared to the Roman Catholic Church or the Russian Orthodox

---

[12] From pages 4 and 5 of the 1923 report as found in Bishop John L. Nuelsen's Archive, Zürich, Switzerland.

[13] At the time these villages were in the Kemerovo region, 350 kilometers east of Novosibirsk.

Church, of course, the MEC Mission in Tsarist Russia was very small, but when one considers that it had only officially begun in the Baltics ca. 1900 and officially initiated in St. Petersburg in 1907, and legally registered there in 1909, its progress and effectiveness were extraordinary.

The advent of the Bolshevik Revolution, of course, made the work of the MEC in Russia proper much more difficult. Properties were confiscated, even if the continued use by previous owners in principle was permitted. In 1918, the Russian government demanded that the superintendent of the MEC work, George A. Simons, leave Russia. He left quite reluctantly, earnestly believing that he would return to resume his work, which was the sincere desire of Sister Anna and all of the coworkers. After a brief stay in the United States, Simons was reassigned to Riga, Latvia, where he hoped to be able to continue the MEC Russian ministries. Sister Anna Eklund was left in charge of the Mission in St. Petersburg and Russia proper.

At the end of the First World War it was most fortunate that a young returning soldier, Russian-Estonian Oskar Pöld, was very interested in entering the Methodist Episcopal ministry. Before he was drafted into military service he had wanted to go to Frankfurt-am-Main to study at the MEC seminary. He arrived in St. Petersburg in March 1921 and immediately began to assist Sister Anna in the work, and in 1922 Pöld was assigned as the pastor in St. Petersburg. Pöld, who was fluent in Russian, Estonian, and German, and had some knowledge of English and Swedish, labored diligently with Sister Anna almost to the final closing of the MEC in that city in 1931, when she finally returned to Finland, never to return to Russia.

Even with Simons' departure the work in Russia continued to grow. A congregation was

MEC building in the city of Novgorod; Sister Anna Eklund with Pastor Tartarinovitch and two members of the congregation

Pastor Tatarinovitch (seated left on the front row) and Sister Anna Eklund (standing, white collar) with members of the Novgorod congregation

begun in Novgorod and one of the assistants in St. Petersburg, Ivan Tartarinovitch, was assigned there as pastor. Sister Anna also oversaw the purchase of a chapel in Jablonitzy, and Pastor Tartarinovitch later assumed the pastoral leadership there, and a new coworker, Pastor Miron Fomitschoff, was engaged for Novgorod. In addition to all of her other work, Sister Anna also opened a summer camp for children in Jablonitzy.

Sister Anna and Pastor Pöld delivering food to the needy

The winters of 1920–21 and 1921–22 were times of terrible famine in Russia. The hunger was unbelievably horrific. Through the American Red Cross Simons was able to send aid from Methodist European Relief to Sister Anna and the congregation in St. Petersburg. A common sight on the streets of St. Petersburg during the winter months of famine was Sister Anna and Pastor Pöld riding on a horse-drawn sleigh, distributing food to the poor.

Because of public remarks Simons had made about the Revolution, the Russian government would not allow him to return to work in Russia. He did manage, however, two visits to Russia in 1921 and 1922. On the second trip he set up a music school in conjunction with the MEC in St. Petersburg. An adult choir and a children's choir were begun under the direction of two professors of the Leningrad Conservatory, Professor Böhme and Madame de Hübbenet. Sister Anna made a number of trips to Moscow trying to procure visas for the adult choir to go to the United States for a tour, but this never was realized.

Left: *Sister Anna and members of the adult choir of the ME Church of Christ Our Savior in St. Petersburg*

Sister Anna Eklund and Pastor Pöld with members of the ME Church of Christ Our Savior in St. Petersburg, 1921

In 1921 the constituency of the ME Church of Christ Our Savior in St. Petersburg numbered around fifty.

Members of the ME Church of Christ Our Savior, St. Petersburg, attending the Russia Mission Conference in Haapsalu, Estonia, 1921

Bishop John L. Nuelsen followed Bishop William Burt with oversight of the Methodist Episcopal area of Europe and North Africa and took up residence in the city of his birth, Zürich, Switzerland. He attended secondary school and college in Karlsruhe and Bremen, Germany, and studied theology at Drew University in Madison, New Jersey (U.S.). In 1889, he became a member of the German Conference of the MEC. After further study at Berlin and Halle, he taught theology, German, and English in the U.S. Nuelsen supervised the Russian work of the MEC from 1912 to 1924 and 1926 to 1927.

John Louis Nuelsen

Nuelsen is mentioned at this point because he was the bishop, so to speak, of transition. His episcopal leadership spanned the period before and after the Bolshevik Revolution, before and after the departure of George A. Simons from St. Petersburg in 1918, the continuing service of Sister Anna Eklund and Oskar Pöld in that city, and Simons' reassignment to the Baltic States as superintendent (at first also over the Russian work). Nuelsen had a great passion for the mission of the MEC among Russian-speaking populations, and he was untiring in his efforts to administrate and support the work efficiently. In addition, he was an effective ecumenical leader, pastor, and scholar.

The Role of the Baltic States

We must return to the Baltic States, for with George A. Simons' new assignment to Riga, Latvia, after his departure from Russia and a brief stay in the US, with Hjalmar Salmi once again as a coworker, and with Sister Anna Eklund still in St. Petersburg, every attempt was made to maintain the ministries in Russia proper. Bishop John Nuelsen was a most helpful advocate of MEC outreach in Russia, as noted by his detailed reports of conferences and trips through Russia during difficult times and under stressful circumstances.

The period between the World Wars was one in which Methodism began to thrive in Lithuania, Latvia, and Estonia. Its growth in these countries is important for the story of early Russian Methodism, because many of the pastors spoke Russian and served Russian-speaking constituencies. In addition, Simons did his best during his tenure in Riga, as superintendent of the Russia Mission Conference and Baltic Mission to maintain contact with Sister Anna Eklund and the work in St. Petersburg, as well as in other parts of Russia proper. As much interaction as possible was sustained between Methodists in the Baltic States and Russia.

In 1921 the organizing session of the Methodist Episcopal Russia Mission Conference and Baltic Mission was held in Haapsalu, Estonia. At this conference three districts were established: (1) Russia District (district superintendent, Hjalmar Salmi), (2) Estonia District (district superintendent, Martin Prikask, (3) Latvia-Lithuania District (district superintendent, Heinrich Holzschuher. George A. Simons was appointed superintendent and treasurer of the Russia Mission Conference and Baltic Mission.

The following appointments were made for the year 1921–1922:

Russia District

Handrovo	Samuel Patjas
Kiev	to be supplied
Mariinsk Circuit	to be supplied (August Karlson)
Moscow	Eugene Grigorjeff
Petrograd	Hjalmar Salmi and V. Rafalowsky
Petrozavodst Circuit	K. J. Örnberg
Repola & Porajärvi	Adam Varonen
Sigolovo	Samuel Patjas
Volosovo	to be supplied (Vassili Täht)

Estonia District

Arensburg Circuit (Kuressaare)	Hans Söte & one to be supplied (E. Raud)
Dorpat (Tartu)	to be supplied
Fellin	to be supplied
Hapsal (Hapsaalu)	to be supplied (A. Mikkoff)
Narva	to be supplied
Pärnu	to be supplied (Karl Kuum)
Reval (Tallinn)	Martin Prikask
Taps (Tapa)	Johannes Karlson
Weisenstein (Paide)	to be supplied
Wesenberg (Rakvere)	Johannes Karlson

Latvia-Lithuania District

Dünaburg (Daugavpils)	to be supplied
Durben (Durbe)	Karl Beike
Hasenpoth (Aizpute)	to be supplied (Jacob Kant)
Kaunas	Alfred Hühn & one to be supplied (Peter Plitzuwait)
Libau (Liepaja) & Grobin (Grobina) Circuit	Fricis Eidins
Niederbartau (Nica) & Ratzau (Rucava)	to be supplied (Fricis Timbers)
Riga — First Church	Alfred Freiberg
— Central Church	Heinrich Holzschuher & John Witt
— Hagensberg (Agenskalns)	Ernst Bahn
Vilnius	to be supplied
Windau (Ventspils)	to be supplied
Virbalis / Kybartai	Rudolph Brennheiser

During 1921–1922, church property was obtained in Riga, Latvia. The imposing four-story Georgian structure on Elisabetes *iela* (street) became the administrative and training center of Methodism in the Baltic States between the World Wars.

Methodist Episcopal Church Building in Riga, which housed the MEC Training Institute, missionary residence, and Central Church, Elisabetes iela 15 (Elizabeth Street 15)

In 1922 the annual meeting of the Methodist Episcopal Russia Mission Conference and Baltic Mission was held in Riga. While Methodism in all three Baltic States thrived between the World Wars, Latvia played a particularly important role. It was there that the *Khristianski*

Pobornik (Russian *Christian Advocate*) was revived and published largely through the efforts of George A. Simons and Hjalmar Salmi. It contains a wealth of information regarding the life and growth of Methodism in the Baltics. At the same time, it is a primary source of knowledge for what was going on in the MEC congregations of Russia, particularly St. Petersburg.

In addition to the *Khristianski Pobornik* there were *Christian Advocates* published in Estonian (*Kristlik Kaitsia*), Latvian (*Kristigs Aisstahwis*), and Lithuanian (*Krikščionystės Sargas*).

George A. Simons' dream of a theological school where students could be educated in the languages of the Baltic States, as well as in Russian and English, was realized with the purchase of the property on Elizabeth Street. This building served as the headquarters of the Russian Mission Conference and Baltic Mission. The MEC Central Church, in which services in four languages were held every Sunday, was on the first floor. In addition, English and French classes, free of charge, met regularly. The superintendent, George A. Simons, lived on the second floor. The Rev. John Witt, Manager of Methodist Child Welfare for the Baltics and Russia, resided on the third floor. The fourth floor was reserved for the Methodist Training Institute, opened in the fall of 1922.

Students and Faculty of the Methodist Training Institute in Riga, Latvia
Seated, left to right: the Rev. von Seck, the Rev. Hans Söte, Dr. George A. Simons, the Rev. A. Röhrich
Second row, left to right: not identified, Mr. Waldman, Mr. Volskis, Mr. Eidins
Third row, left to right: Mr. Burbulys, Mr. Mosienko, Mr. Kviadravečius

The building at Akas Street 13 was purchased in 1921. It was originally built in 1907 by a dedicated Baroness, who was very interested in the Temperance movement. It was here that the first Temperance Society of the Baltics was organized. After her death, the building was purchased by the MEC. In addition to the fine worship space for the congregation, there were two apartments: one for the pastor and one for the leader of MEC work in Russia. It was located in the heart of the city, and its spacious three stories and basement provided ample meeting rooms for worship, education, lodging of the pastor, and humanitarian ministries.

Exterior of Riga First MEC

Interior of Riga First MEC

In Latvia there was a significant Russian-speaking population, and hence, the Bethany MEC for Russian-language ministry was constructed, and one of its first pastors was the Rev. Serge Mosienko, who later became pastor of the MEC in Kaunas, Lithuania, and district superintendent of the Lithuania District.

Bethany MEC, Riga

Under the leadership of Dr. George A. Simons, Sister Anna Eklund, and the Rev. Hjalmar Salmi, strong emphasis was laid on the Wesleyan dimensions of social outreach throughout all geographical areas of the Methodist Episcopal work in the Baltic States and Russia. It should be added that the episcopal leaders with oversight of this work also provided strong support for the humanitarian outreach to the poor and marginalized. In Riga, for example, at the Methodist headquarters building, a warm meal was served once a day to students of the university, who had little or no resources to obtain food for themselves.

Sister Anna's letters and records are filled with accounts of ministry to the poor and hungry of Russia. Some of the most moving accounts of her service come from those who received the benefit of her dedicated service. She sold her own clothes, even her undergarments, to have resources to buy food, medicine, and clothing for persons in need. A member of the St. Petersburg congregation wrote the following words about Sister Anna in a letter dated Nov. 6, 1921:

> It is thirteen years since Sister Anna came to our city in order to work together with our dear Pastor, Dr. Simons, for the benefit of the Russian nation and the glory of God.
>
> She had a hard time at first in this strange place, not knowing even the Russian language, which is not easy for foreigners to learn. But Sister Anna possessed another language—the language of love for suffering mankind. The poor, the sick, and distressed understood her very well. Nationality and creed make no difference. She is one and the same to everybody. Everywhere she goes she wins the hearts of the people through her patience, love, and good temperament. Who does not know Sister Anna? How many poor has she visited, how many sick has she helped, how many unhappy has she comforted, and how many tears has she dried?[14]

Even though Simons could not return officially to work in St. Petersburg, he was indefatigable in the effort to procure food, clothing, and medical supplies for the needy of Russia. He continued to prepare relief efforts through any channel open to him, and his coworker of many years, the Rev. Salmi, was equally active in this work.

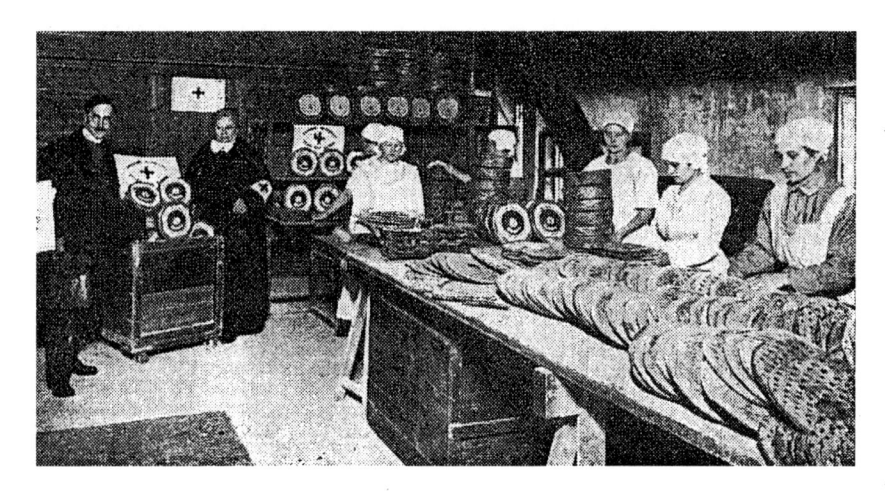

Left: *Sister Anna and Dr. Simons with others preparing a relief shipment for Russia*

This photograph illustrates the untiring relief efforts of Sister Anna and Dr. Simons. Here they are seen in 1921 preparing one of many shipments of the "American Methodist Relief and Child Welfare" for Russia in the warehouse of the Elanto Cooperative Society in Helsinki, Finland. John Witt, a Methodist from Sweden assigned to Latvia, was a resident at the Methodist Episcopal Headquarters in Riga, and among his responsibilities was "Methodist Relief and Child Welfare for the Baltic States and Russia."

Of course, needs were great not only in Russia. Throughout the Baltic States as well, one finds evidence of the same kind of outreach. Just as a children's home was established in Handrovo, Russia. Methodist Episcopal Children's Homes were opened in Tallinn (Estonia) and Riga (Latvia).

---

[14] This is an excerpt from a much longer letter which is signed simply, "A member of the congregation, A. K." See the full letter in this author's book *Sister Anna Eklund (1867–1949): A Methodist Saint in Russia,* pp. 55–57.

Drawing of the MEC Children's Home, Riga, Latvia

The Rev. Hans Söte with Mrs. A. Busch, Matron of the MEC Children's Home in Riga, Latvia,

The building of the Children's Home in Riga was located adjacent to Riga First MEC on Akas Street. The Rev. Hans Söte was assigned the oversight of the MEC Children's Homes in Latvia and Estonia.

Documentation of the plans to establish a Children's Home in the city of Kaunas, Lithuania, was discovered in the National Archives in Vilnius, Lithuania. Property was located, and the transactions for purchase seem to be have been processed, and the structural and administrative organization appears to have been completed. There is no evidence, however, that the Lithuanian counterpart to the Children's Homes in Russia, Estonia, and Latvia, was ever actually realized.

In the three years of existence of the Methodist Episcopal Russian Mission Conference and Baltic Mission the seeds were sown for a number of humanitarian aid programs through channels established within the MEC work of the Baltic States and Russia.

One of the primary concerns of Bishop John L. Nuelen was the leadership of women for these programs. Fortunately a number of young women committed their lives to serve as deaconesses, and some of them were sent to the Bethany Mother House in Hamburg for training and others to the training center at Frankfurt-am-Main. Their service would prove indispensable to the MEC Mission.

It is difficult to imagine how the missions of early Russian Methodism could have thrived without the invaluable contributions of women, particularly in the arenas of health and education, both Christian and secular.

Left: *MEC Children's Home, Tallinn, Estonia*

Left: *The Rev. Hans Söte with [to his right] deaconess, Sister Alice Ködar, Director of the MEC Children's Home in Tallinn, Estonia, and Estonian children living at the Home. Her assistant [far left] is Miss M. Mändeljalg, one of the first members of the MEC in St. Petersburg.*

Baltic and Slavic Mission Conference

In 1923, the Methodist Episcopal Russian Mission Conference and Baltic Mission convened in Kaunas, Lithuania. This was its last meeting, for in 1924 the Baltic and Slavic Mission Conference (henceforth BSMC) was organized.

Bishop John L. Nuelsen's 1922–1923 report titled "Russia" provides an excellent summary of how the work in Russia and the Baltic States had progressed administratively from its beginnings to the formation of the BSMC.

Until the General Conference of 1920 the work in the whole Russian Empire was organized as "Russia Mission." It included the work in Russia proper . . . also two German congregations in Kowno [Kaunas] and Wirballen [Virbalis/Kybartai] near the German frontier, the work among the Estonians on the island of Oesel [Sareemaa] and the beginnings of the work in Riga, Latvia. All the preachers in the Russia Mission were members of the Finland Annual Conference. The Superintendent from the very beginning was the Rev. Geo. A. Simons, formerly of the New York East Conference. The Enabling Act passed by the General Conference of 1912 and reiterated by the General Conference of 1916, permitting the Russia Mission to organize into a Mission Conference, was not taken advantage of until 1920. The General Conference of 1920 in addition to reiterating the enabling act fixed the following boundaries: "Russia Mission shall include the republic of Russia. Baltic Mission shall include the Baltic and Slavic republics contiguous to Russia."

In accordance with the Enabling Act the Russia Mission Conference was organized in July 1921 in Hapsal [Hapsaalu], Estonia, and all the members of Conference working in Russia and in the Baltics were transferred into the newly formed Russia Mission Conference. It was unfortunate that the General Conference made no provision to organize a Baltic Mission Conference. The expectation was that Russia would open soon and that the work in the country would develop more speedily than the Baltic work. However, the political conditions rendering it impossible for any of our workers in Russia to leave their country in order to attend the Conference and it being equally impossible for our preachers in the Baltics to enter Russia, I was compelled to convene the Russia Mission Conference outside of Russia and in the absence of the workers in Russia. Hence, I did not organize a separate Baltic Mission but conducted the business of the Conference under the name of "Russia Mission Conference and Baltic Mission." As a matter of fact, we had no knowledge concerning our brethren in Russia until the year 1922. Among the workers in Russia were no members of Conference, only local preachers, some of whom had been in Frankfurt but were called to military service. The Conference of 1922 met in Riga and Brother Pöld of Petrograd and Sister Anna had received permission from the Russian Government to leave the country for the purpose of attending the Conference. Five Russia brethren were received on trial under the missionary rule. They were continued on trial at the Conference of 1923. Since not one of our preachers in Russia is a member of conference in full connection, I could not, as yet, separate the Baltic Mission from the Russia Mission Conference. The political situation does not make it advisable to continue this arrangement. I shall request the coming General Conference to grant an Enabling Act allowing the Baltic Mission to organize as a Mission Conference. After having admitted the brethren working in Russia into full membership, the two bodies may separate.[15]

After the Enabling Act of the General Conference of 1924, Bishop Anton Bast organized the BSMC on August 27, 1924, independently from the MEC work in Russia, which the General Conference refused to expand. The first meeting of the BSMC took place in Kuressaare on the Island of Sareemaa, Estonia, where Vassili Täht and Karl Kuum had first sown the seeds for Methodism in Estonia and where Martin Prikask had evangelized so effectively. The superintendent, George A. Simons, reported at the Conference that on the island there were ninety-five preaching places, thirty-two local preachers, a membership of 366, and thousands of Methodist friends.

MEC leadership hoped that the work in the Baltic States would provide an avenue for training Russian workers for the MEC mission in Russia proper, as the political situation there had increasingly become more difficult and there seemed no likelihood of viable training options within Russia itself. This viewpoint is understandable, for at the BSMC of 1924, forty-six

---

[15] John L. Nuelsen, unpublished "Report on Russia: To the Executive Committee of the Board of Foreign Missions of the Methodist Episcopal Church (1922–1923)," pp. 6–7.

appointments and 150 preaching places were reported. This was no small achievement, since the MEC work in the Baltic States had only begun ca. 1900.

*The first MEC building in Estonia
built at Kuressaare on the Island of Sareema
and consecrated in 1912; site of the first annual meeting
of the BSMC in 1924*

Bishop John Nuelsen reported in 1924 that there were fifteen pastors working in Estonia, fifteen in Latvia, eight in Lithuania, and six were responsible for Russian-language work. It should be noted that while many of the pastors in the Baltic States were fluent in the Russian language, most of the ministries were conducted in the indigenous languages. The two exceptions were in Lithuania and Latvia. In the former, services in Kaunas and Kybartai were at first in German, and in the latter, as noted above, the Bethany MEC in Riga was established specifically for Russian-language ministries. In Estonia official Russian-language work did not begin until 1957. It was initiated by the Rev. Alexander Kuum after his return from imprisonment in Siberia.

Of course, there were many Russian refugees who fled Russia because of the Bolshevik Revolution and the great famine of 1921–1922, and where possible, especially with those Baltic pastors who spoke Russian, there was outreach among them.

It is interesting to follow the annual reports of the Board of Foreign Missions regarding the Russia mission of the MEC. As already noted, 1923 was the final year of the Russia Mission Conference and Baltic Mission. That year the Board of Foreign Missions report had a very brief entry titled "Russia Mission Conference" followed by one paragraph which is hardly a report on the Russia Mission:

Bishop Nuelsen held both the Russia Mission Conference and the Baltic Mission simultaneously in Hapsaalu, Estonia, July 28–31, 1921. The General Conference of 1924 continued the Russia Mission Conference in the Zürich Area, and included the Baltic Mission in the Copenhagen Area. The appointments in Russia are Handrovo, Jamberg circuit, Kiev, Mariinsk circuit, Moscow, Novgorod, Petrograd, Petrozavodsk circuit, Sigolovo, Sinjavino, Tsarskoye Selo, Trotzki and Witebsk.[16]

As late as 1928, the Russia Mission Conference is listed in the report of the Board of Foreign Missions of the MEC. The single paragraph devoted to it lists the area of square miles covered by the country of Russia and the population. Two sentences state the following: "Methodist Episcopal work was begun in Kovauber in 1889 by the Rev. B. A. Carlson from Helsingfors. By appointment of Bishop Burt in 1907 the work was organized under Rev. G. A. Simons." The appointments are no longer listed; rather the report states simply: "There are fifteen pastoral charges."[17]

The BSMC would continue until 1939, its last meeting before the Russian invasion of the Baltic States in 1940. The MEC Mission in Russia would continue until 1931, when Sister Anna Eklund departed Russia for the last time. With Pastor Pöld she had struggled to keep the work going in St. Petersburg and the surrounding villages of Handrovo, Sigolovo, and Haitolovo, as well as in Novgorod and Jablonitzy.

Bishop Nuelsen had oversight of the Russia Mission from 1912 to 1924 and from 1926 to 1927. He made a number of trips into Russia before and after the Revolution, and his reports and letters to Sister Anna Eklund and George A. Simons are a rich source of information regarding the situation there, both the hardships and progress of the mission.

The Deaconess Movement

As we have seen from the beginnings of Methodism in Russia, with the appointment of Sister Anna Eklund a strong deaconess movement emerged. In Russia proper and the Baltic States she was, in large measure, the strength and motivation for it. Many of the women from Russia and the Baltics completed their training at the Bethany Mother House in Hamburg, Germany, or at the Training Center in Frankfurt. The three photographs shown here punctuate the presence and importance of the deaconesses and their work in Russia and the Baltic States. They provided the seminal work of the Mission with women, children, and youth. Without them much of the educational and health services would have been impossible.

Bishop Blake, Simons, and BSMC deaconesses; Ottilie Simons is in the second row center

---

[16] *Annual Report of the Board of Foreign Missions of the Methodist Episcopal Church* (New York: Board of Foreign Missions, 1923), p. 582. Most likely the list of appointments is not accurate.

[17] *Annual Report of the Board of Foreign Missions of the Methodist Episcopal Church* (New York: Board of Foreign Missions, 1928), p. 330.

Bishop John Nuelsen, George A. Simons, BSMC delegates, and deaconesses

Bishop Edgar Blake, George A. Simons, BSMC delegates, and deaconesses

The work of the deaconesses and other women was indispensable to the outreach of early Russian Methodism. Their work with children and youth, especially in the orphanages or in a home for unwed mothers, was tireless and life-giving. After Dr. George A. Simons' departure from St. Petersburg in 1918, Sister Anna Eklund served, for all practical purposes according to Bishop Nuelsen, as the "superintendent" of Methodist work in Russia. With her able assistant, Oskar Pöld, she fought "as a lion" to keep the ME Church of Christ Our Savior open until 1931, when she finally had to return to her home country of Finland.

Mention should also be made of Sister Berta Engels, who was a deaconess of the *Evangelische Gemeinschaft* (Evangelical Church) of Latvia. For almost ten years she served as the deaconess assigned to Kuldiga, but without a pastor. Hence, Sister Berta essentially functioned as the pastor of the congregation there during those years before women were ordained to ministry. The Soviets sent her to Siberia, which she miraculously survived, and afterwards returned to Latvia.

Conclusion

The photographs in this section of the book aid in telling the marvelous and tragic story of early Methodism in Russia and the Baltic States. While the latter were a part of Imperial Russia, Methodism emerged in its own right in the indigenous languages of the countries of Lithuania, Latvia, and Estonia, though Russian was spoken as well. While Methodism in Russia proper had only a brief period in which to flower before the Bolshevik Revolution, it demonstrated the strength of the Wesleyan tradition to minister to the whole person.

In the Baltic States the story was very different. Methodism indeed blossomed between World War I and World War II, and enjoyed twenty years of amazing growth and development. Except in Estonia, however, Methodism was crushed by the onslaught of the Soviets and the reign of totalitarian communism in the 1940s. It survived only in Estonia, but with grave difficulties. Two small house groups of Methodists survived also in Ukraine near the Hungarian border in the towns of Kamenic and Uzhgorod, but to date this author has discovered no photographic documentation of these two congregations.

It is now important to turn to another crucial chapter of early Russian Methodism, namely, the Siberia-Manchuria Mission of the Methodist Episcopal Church, South.

The Methodist Episcopal Church, South
The Siberia-Manchuria Mission

There is another part of the story of Russian Methodism, which has to do with the mission of the MECS in Russian Siberia and Harbin (Manchuria), China. This story involves Russians and two groups of ethnic Koreans: Russian-Koreans who were descendants of ancestors, who, in the mid-nineteenth century, had migrated north to farm the rich land of the Primorski Krai area of Russian Siberia, and Koreans who had fled north after the Japanese invasion of the Korean peninsula in 1910. Of the 1,400,000 Koreans who had migrated north for economic and political reasons, it was estimated that some 5,000 were Methodists. Hence, it was the desire of fellow Methodists in Korea to send them missionaries to aid in establishing their own churches and schools for educating their children. The idea for the mission was officially born in September 1919.

> After the closing of the Korean Annual Conference in Wonsan, Korea, September, 1919, Bishop Lambuth held the Mission meeting at the Wonsan Beach the next day. At that time he was informed of the great needs and opportunities in Siberia and Manchuria where a great multitude of Koreans have migrated since 1870. He was very much interested in it and ordered Rev. M. B. Stokes and J. S. Ryang to visit Siberia at once in view to opening missionary work for Koreans in that section. But that party never went, because the state department at Washington would not issue passport[s] on Siberia at that time.[18]

At the annual meeting of the Board of Missions of the MECS in May 1920, Bishop Walter Russell Lambuth recommended that the opening of the Siberia-Manchuria Mission be authorized. His recommendation was approved, and the following resolution was passed: "Resolved: that in view of the conditions demanding our ministry in that section, we authorize the bishop in charge of the Oriental fields to open work in Siberia."[19]

While Vladivostok fell to the Bolsheviks in March 1918, they were driven back in June of the same year by Czech soldiers aided by Japanese, British, and American troops. Interestingly, 1918 was the year of the founding of the MECS Centenary fund for missions, which eventually would make possible the opening of the Siberia-Manchuria Mission.

During the Korea Annual Conference in September 1920, meeting in Seoul, Korea, Bishop Lambuth appointed the Rev. Dr. W. G. Cram as superintendent of the Siberia-Manchuria Mission and the Rev. Chung Chai Duk, a Korean minister, as a missionary to the new mission. In the following month of October Dr. Cram, the Rev. Chung Chai Duk, and the Rev. J. S. Ryang traveled to Siberia and Manchuria. The Rev. Chung was assigned to begin the work among Koreans in Kirin and the surrounding area. The Rev. Ryang visited Chang Chun, Kirin, and Harbin in Chinese Manchuria, and Nikolsk-Ussurisk and Vladivostok in Russian Siberia.

Bishop Walter R. Lambuth

---

[18] See the anonymous article, "The Historical Facts of the Siberia-Manchuria Mission," *The Missionary Voice* (August 1922), p. 231.

[19] Ibid.

Not only was Bishop Lambuth interested in reaching the emigrant Korean population in Russian Siberia and Manchuria, he was deeply interested in reaching Russians with the Christian gospel. At the time of the opening of the MECS Siberia-Manchuria Mission the city of Harbin in Manchuria had one of the largest European emigrant communities in Asia. There were some 100,000 Russians and Poles in the city, in addition to Koreans, Japanese, and, of course, the indigenous Chinese population. Hence, it is easy to see why Russian Siberia and Manchuria were the two important foci of the new mission.

After the first exploratory journey for the new mission was made in October 1920 the Korean ministry assignments were as follows: the Rev. Chung, as noted, to the Kirin area and the Rev. Ryang to Valdivostok and Nikolsk-Ussurisk in Russian Siberia.

The Rev. Chung moved forward rapidly with the mission in Kirin, and by November 1920 he had established the first Korean congregation with fifteen members and nearby had begun another.

Russian Siberia

The year 1921 was an amazingly active year for the Mission. Korean congregations were founded in Harbin and smaller surrounding villages. In March the first Korean congregation was begun in Russian Siberia with about fifty persons in Nikolsk-Ussurisk, north of Vladivostok in the Primorski Krai. In April the superintendent, Dr. Cram, reported the addition of some 500 new members in Siberia and Manchuria. In June, Cram and Ryang made a second missionary journey to Chang Chun, Kirin, Harbin, Nikolsk-Ussurisk, and Vladivostok. In July Bishop Lambuth traveled to Siberia with Dr. Cram, the Rev. J. O. J. Taylor, the Rev. L. C. Brannan, and the Rev. Ryang, visiting Mukden, Chang Chun, Kirin, and Harbin in Manchuria, and Nikolsk-Ussurisk and Vladivostok in Russian Siberia.

From July 31 to August 1, 1921, the First Annual Meeting of the Siberia-Manchuria Mission was held in Nikolsk-Ussurisk in the MECS Church with Bishop Lambuth presiding. By this time a Methodist mission compound had been established there. Buildings were procured and outfitted for worship and schools for children. The rapidity with which a school for boys and a school for girls were established was amazing. With the influx of emigrants, however, there were many qualified teachers available, who were delighted to find employment, even at low salaries.

It was reported that two ordained Korean clergy and twelve Korean helpers had organized thirty groups with 224 full members, a constituency of 1,261, and eleven Sunday Schools with twenty teachers and 630 pupils. One hundred fifty members were reported for the Nikolsk-Ussurisk congregation.

J. S. Ryang, W. G. Cram, Bishop Lambuth, Chung Chai Duk

In Nikolsk-Ussurisk at this time there were about 5,000 Korean inhabitants and in Vladivostok about 15,000. The Minutes of the Annual Meeting (1921) of the Mission included the following statement: "It was decided that the center of our operations should be from the two cities of Vladivostok and Nikolsk and that we should lay great stress on the immediate advance into the Ussuri valley region." [20]

Part of the MECS Mission complex in Nikolsk-Ussurisk, see p. 92

MECS building and congregation in Nikolsk-Ussurisk, see p. 92.

---

[20] *First Annual Meeting of the Siberia-Manchuria Mission of the Methodist Episcopal Church, South* (Nikolsk-Ussurisk, Siberia, July 31–August 1, 1921), p. 11.

Pupils from the Boys' School at Nikolsk-Ussurisk with Teachers

Pupils from the Girls' School at Nikolsk-Ussurisk with Teachers

Korean MECS Congregation in Nikolsk-Ussurisk, 1921

The Second Annual Meeting of the Siberia-Manchuria Mission was convened October 10–12, 1922, in Vladivostok, only two weeks before the Bolsheviks would march into the city on October 25 and take over. By October 1922, the Vladivostok MECS Church was near completion, and the Annual Meeting was held there with Bishop Hiram A. Boaz presiding. The building was constructed by the Russian builders Pestrikoff and Naamen in less than a year from the time of the property purchase, and was located on Habarovskaya Street. By the time of the Second Annual Meeting the missionary family of George and Vada Erwin and their three children had arrived

MECS Building, Vladivostok

in Vladivostok. The Rev. Erwin and another newly assigned missionary, the Rev. J. O. J. Taylor, were to have worked in Vladivostok, but they would soon be assigned to "Russian Work" in Harbin.

The Minutes of the Second Annual Meeting of the Siberia-Manchuria Mission stated that the Third Annual Meeting would also be convened in Nikolsk-Ussurisk. This never transpired, however, because of the increasingly difficult political situation.

Vladivostok and the Primorski Krai Region

By the time the Bolsheviks took over Vladivostok on October 25, 1922, many people of means had already fled the city and region. George Erwin and family remembered being perhaps the only Americans left in the city, and they recalled watching the bedraggled Bolshevik army march wearily up the hill in front of the apartment where they were living, only to be well dressed four days later after plundering the city. Within a short time church properties were confiscated, and a difficult period for Christians began.

Bishop Hiram A. Boaz

The rapidity with which the work of the Siberia-Manchuria Mission moved forward has already been noted. By the summer of 1922 a Bible Training

No. 35 Pushkinskaya Street in Vladivostok where the Erwins lived in an apartment

School was held in Nikolsk-Ussurisk with thirty-nine participants.

The institutional and organizational evidence alone of the MECS Russian Siberia part of the Mission underscores the amazing and rapid growth of the Mission. By 1922 schools for boys and girls were established in both Vladivostok and Nikolsk-Ussurisk, and four districts of the Siberia-Manchuria Mission had been organized: three in Russian Siberia (Vladivostok, Yernchoo, and Nikolsk), and one in China (North Kondo).

The Missionaries

The Rev. George F. Erwin

Mrs. Vada Erwin

The Rev. J. O. J. Taylor

1922 New Member Class, Vladivostok

The Rev. Kim Young Hak was appointed as pastor in Vladivostok. Even though the Mission Board would soon move the Mission officially to Harbin after the Bolshevik takeover of Russian Siberia, the Rev. Kim would remain in this assignment until 1929.

Before the Bolshevik march on Vladivostok, church membership was steadily increasing. The membership roll of the MECS congregation in Vladivostok may be found in the State Historical Archives of the city of Vladivostok and reflects this growth. It is interesting that at the outset almost all of the names on the roll were Korean, but as

Vladivostok congregation with Bishop Lambuth, W. G. Cram, and J. O. J. Taylor

the church grew, gradually more and more Russian names appeared. Hence, it is clear that the Mission's outreach to the Russians was also effective.

The rapidity of the growth of the Siberia-Manchuria Mission has already been mentioned, but a brief review of the main steps in this swift progress will punctuate this amazing development:[21]

- May 1920: The Board of Missions of the MECS officially authorizes the Siberia-Manchuria Mission.
- Sept. 1920: The first missionaries are appointed: the Rev. Dr. W. G. Cram, as superintendent of the Siberia-Manchuria Mission, the Rev. Chung Chai Duk, as missionary at large for the Mission.
- Oct. 1920: The first missionary journey: On October 5, the following persons depart for Siberia and Manchuria: the Rev. Dr. W. G. Cram, the Rev. Chung Chai Duk, the Rev. J. S. Ryang; places visited: Kirin, Chang Chun, Harbin in Manchuria, and Nikolsk and Vladivostok in Russian Siberia.
- Nov. 1920: The first congregation (Korean) is established in Kirin (Manchuria).
- Jan. 1921: A congregation (Korean) is begun in Harbin (Manchuria) and in a few other places.
- Mar. 1921: First congregation (Korean) is organized in Nikolsk-Ussurisk (Russian Siberia) with about fifty people.
- Apr. 1921: By this date it is reported that the church members of the Siberia-Manchuria Mission number ca. 5,000.
- June 1921: The second missionary journey: the Rev. Dr. Cram and the Rev. Ryang visit Chang Chun, Kirin, Harbin, Nikolsk, and Vladivostok.
- July 1921: Bishop Lambuth with the Rev. Dr. Cram, the Rev. J. O. J. Taylor, the Rev. L. C.

---

[21] See "The Historical Facts of the Siberia-Manchuria Mission," *The Missionary Voice*, Aug. (1922), p. 231.

	Brannan, and the Rev. J. S. Ryang travel to Mukden, Chang Chun, Kirin, Harbin, Nikolsk and Vladivostok.
Aug. 1921:	The first Annual Meeting of the Mission is convened at the MECS compound in Nikolsk-Ussurisk, and the Rev. J. O. J. Taylor opens a Mission office in Vladivostok.
Sept. 1921:	Prof. H. W. Jenkins and family arrive in Harbin, as he has been appointed by Bishop Lambuth as missionary in charge of the Russian work.
Nov. 1921:	Mission Board visit: before his death Bishop Lambuth had requested a visit from the Board of Missions. Dr. F. S. Parker, general secretary of the Epworth League and member of the Board of Missions, visits the Siberia-Manchuria Mission.
Dec. 1921:	First Training Institute is conducted from Dec. 2 to 9 by the Rev. J. S. Ryang and the Rev. Chung Chai Duk with sixteen preachers and one Bible woman attending.
Feb. 1922:	It is reported that eighty congregations have been established with a constituency of 3,208.
May 1922:	The boundaries of the Siberia-Manchuria Mission are defined as follows by the General Conference meeting in Hot Springs: "The Siberia Mission shall include Siberia and the work among Koreans and Russians in Manchuria."[22]

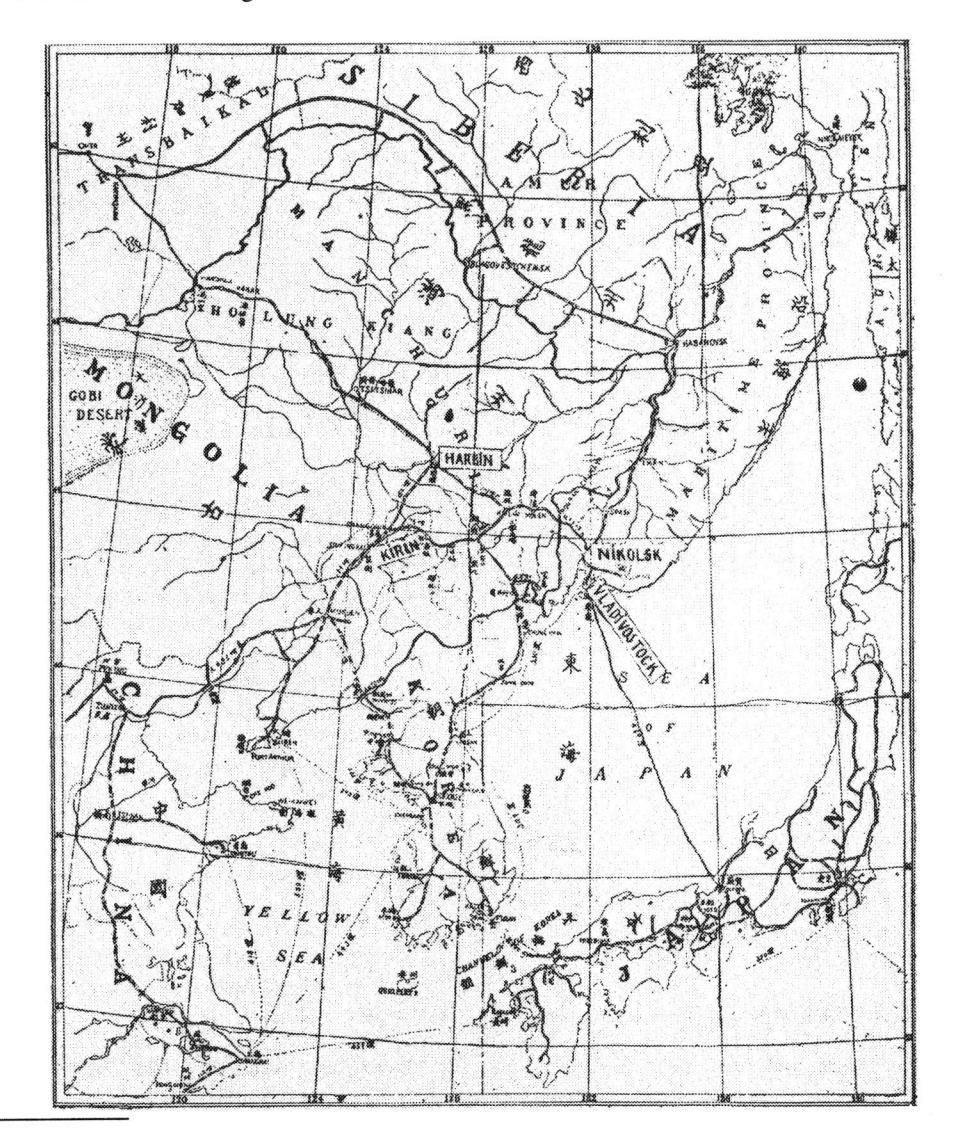

---

[22] Ibid.

May 1922: The missionaries, the Rev. George Erwin, his wife Vada, and children arrive in Vladivostok.
Oct. 1922: Vladivostok falls to the Bolsheviks.
Feb. 1923: The Erwin family departs for Harbin and is followed shortly thereafter by the Taylor family. By the spring Russian Methodist work is concentrated in Harbin.[23]

Russian-Language Work in Harbin, China

Before and after the Bolshevik takeover of Russian Siberia many Russians and Koreans fled into Manchuria. As already noted, there was a large Russian population in Harbin, as well as Koreans and Japanese. Many Russians had gone out to Manchuria to work on the trans-Siberian railway and had settled, if only temporarily, in the largest cosmopolitan Manchurian city, Harbin, on the railway. Others had come there in the early years of the Bolshevik Revolution, having fled from Russia proper. Hence, there was a tremendously large emigrant community.

Professor H. W. Jenkins had already been assigned as superintendent of the Siberia-Manchuria Mission and in charge of Russian work. With the move of missionaries from Vladivostok, the Rev. George Erwin and his wife, Vada, were now added to the Harbin staff. Jenkins had been diligent in his preparations for the MECS Mission in Harbin and surrounding area. It should be added that in addition to the Russian work Methodist churches had been established for Koreans, Japanese, and Chinese. Within a short period of time property was procured on Telinskaya Street and a fine building, known as the Methodist Institute, was equipped for lodging and teaching. It was the missionary residence and provided classrooms for a variety of vocational and professional learning, e.g., bookkeeping, English and Russian typewriting, English language.

The progress of this part of the Siberia-Manchuria Mission is one of the most phenomenal in Methodist mission history.

What was accomplished in a span of six to seven years seems almost impossible, but the evidence is clear, as will be seen in the reports and photographs that follow.

Prof. H. W. Jenkins

---

[23] Even though the Mission and all missionary personnel were officially moved by the spring of 1923 to Harbin (Manchuria) from Russian Siberia, the MECS congregations in Vladivostok and Nikolsk-Ussurisk continued to function until 1929 under the most difficult of circumstances. Their properties were confiscated by the communists, and the options for holding worship and other gatherings were increasingly limited by the authorities. See this author's article, "Methodism in Russian Siberia, 1920–1929," *Methodist History,* 36:3(April 1998): 153–161. Bishop Boaz reported in 1918 the following: "The atheistic Bolsheviks have molested the work there [Vladivostok District] in no small way. We had a good church building, which they have confiscated and made into a clubroom and dance hall. The preacher [the Rev. Kim Young Hak] and the people were driven out at the point of a pistol and the women insulted. The preacher was arrested and put in jail for no other reason than being a preacher of the gospel and hesitating to surrender his house of worship to the Soviets. The Soviets are doing all they can to stamp out the Christian religion." "Our Siberia Mission," *Missionary Voice*, October (1925): 295.

The Rev. George F. Erwin was assigned as pastor of Central Church of the MECS in Harbin. He has provided an excellent summary of the beginning and continuance of the Russian ministries in Harbin:

> On the evening of May 6, 1923, in the basement of the mission house at Telinskaya Street No. 128, the first Methodist Church service for Russians was held. Very little notice had been given of this first meeting, but about thirty people came. From Sunday to Sunday our congregation grew until we saw the need of getting a larger hall.
>
> Bishop Boaz came to us in September. While he was here we secured our new building at 175 Garinskay Street, where he preached several times to a well-filled house. The Bishop made the first effort at organizing the people into a Methodist Church. With the first opportunity given for membership twenty-six people came forward and asked for admission. These members were divided between the Central Church and Modyagow.
>
> Just a few weeks after the [Central] Church was opened in New Town, we opened a second one at 29 Gogalifskaya Street in Modyagow under the direction of N. J. Pöysti, pastor.[24]
>
> The work in both places has grown far beyond our fondest expectations. We have in the two churches more than one hundred full members and some on the waiting list. Besides many members, we have many visitors at each church service. Most of the time our halls are crowded.
>
> The coming of J. R. Moose and M. B. Stokes from our Korea Mission to assist in our revival meetings was a great spiritual uplift to us all. We feel that our whole mission was greatly strengthened by the strong evangelistic preaching which they did. We shall long remember them for the examples of godliness which they demonstrated in their lives while in our midst.
>
> In both of the above-named churches we have very active Sunday schools and Epworth Leagues where the people learn how to become active Christian workers. We also have in each of these churches well-attended prayer meetings. Our members are urged to attend these meetings regularly.
>
> We now have a new church at Pristan, corner of Diagnallnaya and Pekarnaya Streets—No. 48 Diagnallnaya. The first service was held in December 1923. In just a short while after the opening, Brothers Stokes and Moose held a very successful series of meetings there which were very well attended. Many people gave their names as probationers or students of the principles of Methodism. An active Sunday school is now held there each Sunday. This church is under the pastorate of G. I. Yasinitsky and B. M. Venogradoff, but is under the direct supervision of Prof. H. W. Jenkins.
>
> We are not making a fight on other churches. We see many things in them that the Bible does not justify, but we are giving the people the right of choice. If they are not satisfied with what one church teaches about religion and come to us and say that they do not get satisfaction out of their mother church, then I think that they should have the privilege of Methodism. Methodism has been a blessing to people all over the world. Since it has been a blessing to so many other people, I believe that it can be a blessing to the Russian people.[25]

In Manchuria the primary location of Methodism was in Harbin. Outreach was developed rapidly in three sections of the city: New Town, Pristan, and Modyagow. Churches were established in all three. New Town was the heart of the city and at a higher elevation than the other two sections. It was primarily residential, and many of its inhabitants were well-paid railway employees and foreigners, particularly Americans and English. By 1924, the New Town

---

[24] This is the same Finnish-born N. J. Pöysti, who worked with the MEC in St. Petersburg, and spoke fluent Russian.

[25] George F. Erwin, "A Review of Our Church Work in Harbin," *The Missionary Voice,* Sept. (1924): 270.

Church was having a weekly attendance at worship of two to three hundred and a Sunday school attendance of 125.

Pristan was the city's center of commerce. Its many railroad shops employed between eight and ten thousand Russians. The congregation in this part of the city was begun in December 1923 under the leadership of the young Russian pastor, Gregory I. Yasinitsky. By the fall of 1924 attendance at weekly worship was averaging 150 and the Sunday school seventy-five.

The Modyagow section of Harbin was populated mainly by middle-class Russians from a variety of occupations. By the fall of 1924, attendance at weekly worship of the Modyagow Church averaged between three and four hundred and the Sunday School about eighty.

Missionary Residence and Methodist Institute, Telenskaya Street, Harbin

There follows a series of photographs which illustrate the extent of the Russian work of the MECS in Harbin. Not only were congregations established and buildings procured and equipped for worship and education; schools were also opened which rapidly gained a reputation as some of the finest educational institutions in Harbin in spite of the frequent lack of needed supplies.

By 1924–1925, schools had been opened in New Town (Central MECS School) and Pristan (Pristan MECS School). The former enrolled 387 children and youth in nine classes, and enrollment in the latter reached 206, for a total of 593 in both schools. In 1926–1927, two more classes were added at Central, giving it a total of ten grades. Chapel services and Bible study were included along with general studies.

The educational opportunities provided through the Mission were characteristic of a Wesleyan perspective which sought to minister to the whole person. Hence, the Mission opened a clinic in connection with the church in Modyagow. What better symbol could there have been for a church in the Wesleyan tradition than the signs on the same building which said "Methodist Episcopal Church" and "Methodist Episcopal Church Ambulatory Clinic"?

There was an increasing and pressing need for medical assistance. The options for health care in Harbin for the extremely large number of poor people, the indigenous Chinese population, and the thousands of emigrants were gravely limited. At the clinic opened by the MECS medicines were dispensed at half the price of purchase in a retail drug store. Given the limited incomes of the population, and thousands who had almost nothing, it is not surprising that the demand for medications at the clinic climbed steadily. This meant that the clinic had to expand its stock of medicines, which it was only able to do through the support of churches in the U.S. and the Centenary fund.

Building in which the MECS Modyagow Church and Ambulatory Clinic were located

From June 1924 to June 1925, the number of treatments at the clinic totaled 22,564 for 4,219 patients. In September of 1925, the clinic took over the medical and dental work of the two MECS schools, which included over 500 students. Fortunately many of the Russian emigrants were very well educated, and two of the Russian doctors, Dr. Uspensky and Dr. Serebriakoff, were of tremendous assistance to the clinic. It was one of the most desired centers for medical assistance in Harbin at this time and word spread widely of this unique outreach of the Methodist Episcopal Church, South Siberia-Manchuria Mission.

Left: *New Town MECS Church and School*

Members of the Sunday School and Teachers, MECS Central Church

Left: *Central MECS School, Primary Grades*

Central MECS School, Intermediate Grades

Central MECS School, Upper Grades

Pupils and Teachers of Central MECS School

Bishop Boaz (center second row) with Teachers and Pupils of the Pristan MECS School

Another school was opened by the Siberia-Manchuria Mission in the Pristan section of Harbin, in the heart of the city.

Left: *Pristan MECS School, Intermediate Grades*

The following fascinating collage of photographs of Bishop Boaz, MECS missionaries, and the teachers at the Central MECS Gymnasium (High School) for the academic year 1925–1926 was produced in a poster format.

In addition to the elementary and secondary schools, Jenkins, Erwin, and Pöysti began the training of pastors for Russian-language ministry at the Methodist Institute. Soon an impressive group of young Russians were studying for the ministry and serving as pastors and pastoral assistants in the mission: G. I. Yasinitsky, A. F. Gavrilovchuk, A. A. Guroff, G. V. Volegoff, K. D. Egoroff, and B. M. Venogradoff.

At the MECS Bible Institute in Harbin some of the first indigenous Russian pastors were trained for ministry. In addition to the study of the Bible, they pursued a broad spectrum of courses including Church History taught by George F. Erwin and Systematic Theology taught by John C. Hawk, a MECS missionary working with the Chinese in Harbin. Courses were also offered in homiletics, New Testament, and the Old Testament prophets.

All of the young Russian student pastors had an opportunity to be engaged in active pastoral ministry. A. F. Gavrilovchuk served as the Assistant Pastor of Central MECS Church. G. I. Yasinitsky and B. M. Venogradoff were assigned as the pastors of the congregation in Pristan and G. V. Volegoff as assistant pastor. Yasinitsky also taught Bible in the MECS schools of Harbin. The Rev. N. J. Pöysti, who taught and assisted with Russian translation at the MECS

Bible Institute, served as the pastor of the Modyagow congregation. The Rev. George F. Erwin was appointed the pastor of the Central MECS congregation.

Students and Faculty of the MECS Training Institute, Harbin
Front row, left to right: Guroff, Pöysti, Jenkins, Bishop Boaz, Erwin, Yasinitsky

The First Indigenous Russian Pastors in Harbin

G. I. Yasinitsky   *A. F. Gavrilovchuk*   *A. A. Guroff*

G. V. Volegoff  *K. D. Egoroff*  *B. M Venogradoff*

Unfortunately Mr. Venogradoff died unexpectedly of heart disease on February 24, 1924, and was buried by the MECS Mission two days later. He was born in an Orthodox family in St. Petersburg, educated there in a gymnasium, and served in the Russian military during the Russo-German War. Later Venogradoff went to Vladivostok and attended the university. After completing his studies, he worked for the YMCA. Later he arrived in Harbin and became acquainted with the work of the MECS and decided to dedicate his life to God's service. He then entered the MECS Bible School of the Methodist Institute and did very well in his studies. Bishop Boaz then assigned him to work in the Pristan MECS Church, where he served until his untimely death.

Bishop Boaz (center) and first deacons ordained by the Mission: Guroff (left), Yasinitsky (right)

The Rev. George F. Erwin was director of evangelism for the Siberia-Manchuria Mission. At the 1925 Annual Meeting of the Russia Department of the Mission it was decided to open a new church outside of Harbin along the Chinese Eastern Railroad. The station of Tsitsihar, located on the western line of the railroad, was selected as the site. Tsitsihar was about 200 miles from Harbin and about twenty miles from the old Chinese city bearing the same name. It was then the capital of the most northern province of China. A. A. Guroff, pictured on the previous page, was designated at the Annual Meeting to serve this congregation. He had a most interesting background, as related by George F. Erwin: "Brother Guroff, who is a graduate of a Russian Military Academy in Siberia, served as an officer during the Russian Revolution, and after the fall of the old Russian party, he and his family made their way to Harbin as refugees. He became a janitor for one of our Churches and was converted. He was admitted into our Bible school, where he proved to be an excellent Bible student and became a prospective pastor."[26]

Tsitsihar Congregation with Pastors Guroff and Gavrilovchuk kneeling in the front row

After making acquaintances throughout the Russian community and converting an old storehouse into an appropriate meeting and teaching space, the MECS work officially began in Tsitsihar on December 27, 1925.

The Rev. Erwin reported on his trip to Tsitsihar at the beginning of 1926 as follows:

> On January 10 Brother A. Gavrilovchuk, my assistant pastor at Central Church, and I went to visit the work at Tsitsihar, expecting to stay and preach for a day or two. We found that the interest grew from day to day, and we stayed for eight days instead of the original one or two. I preached thirteen times. The hall was nearly always full, and sometimes even all standing room was taken, and many were turned away because they could not get into the house. I think that this was the first time that many of them ever heard a sermon such as we preach. At the last service thirty hands went up when I asked how many would like to join an instruction class.[27]

Pastor Guroff soon began an Epworth League (the MECS youth organization) and a Sunday school. By June of 1926, the former had sixty members and the membership instruction class had grown to the same number.

The combination of creative missionaries and indigenous Russian pastoral leadership, as can be seen from the above photographs, produced amazing results in the emigrant Russian community of Harbin and outlying area. In the context of the wide expanse of Russian Siberia and Manchuria the number of participants may seem miniscule, but it should be emphasized that the Mission in Russian Siberia existed only for a span of nine years (1920–1929) and in Man-

---

[26] "Opening New Work in Manchuria," *Missionary Voice,* June (1926): 10 (170).

[27] Ibid.

churia for seven years (1920–1927). The enthusiasm, commitment, and faithfulness of the Russians in Harbin and Tsitsihar and of the Korean constituency in Vladivostok and Nikolsk-Ussurisk cannot be overstated. Their commitment to the Triune God and the church inaugurated by Jesus Christ was unswerving.

The photograph below was taken at Central Church in February of 1926, when a Wesleyan Love Feast was celebrated by members of the Harbin MECS congregations. There were 177 persons in attendance.

Love Feast at MECS Central Church in Harbin

Women's Work

On October 19, 1923, two new missionaries, Constance Rumbough and Lillian Wahl, arrived in Harbin, having been sent by the Women's Council of the Woman's Missionary Society of the MECS. They immediately began the study of the Russian language, spending at least five to six hours a day in private tutoring classes and personal study. They advanced very quickly. In addition to their language study, they were able to help with other work of the mission. Rumbough taught biblical courses at the Methodist Institute for the ministerial studies and worked to develop the programs of the Woman's Missionary Society and the Epworth League. She oversaw the joint effort of the women in Central Church and the Modyagow Church to support a Bible woman in the Chinese Methodist Church in Harbin. Rumbough concluded her annual report of 1923–1924 to the Annual Meeting of the Mission with these words: "My first year of missionary work has been filled with study and

Constance Rumbough    *Lillian Wahl*

work. It has brought two blessings—an acquaintance and love for the Russian people, and a sense of a deeper and abiding fellowship with God."[28]

Lillian Wahl was also involved with the development of the Woman's Missionary Society. At first the women were meeting only once a month, but as their work grew from April 1924 onward they met once a week. They were not only involved with Bible study and prayer but with gathering clothing and food for the poor. In her annual report to the Mission Miss Wahl related that they had helped twenty-five people find employment during the course of the year. She also encouraged the Epworth League to follow the example of the women and provide some assistance to the poor.

Wahl concluded her report to the Annual Meeting of the Mission by saying: "It has been a real joy to work and help in every possible way and to see the great possibilities of our people and help them to realize them. The greatest thing is to see the people accept Jesus Christ as their personal Saviour and give themselves in service unto him."[29]

The work of these two women was extraordinary. By early 1925, they were able to teach in Russian. They were working with orphans, organizing and leading summer camps for women, girls, and boys. Their work for and among the poor was unending. They helped the women to arrange concerts, which aided the raising of funds to buy Russian books for the library of the Mission. They were extremely intentional about empowering indigenous Russian leadership. For example, they organized a Junior League for the protection of children with a Russian woman named Bradovitch in charge, who worked diligently and faithfully. They arranged weekly programs with Russian speakers, such as one on the religions of China presented by Mr. Skurkin, a teacher at the Commercial School of Harbin.

Publications

On July 15, 1923, the Mission printed the first issue of the *Khristianski Pobornik* (*The Christian Advocate*). This is same name of a similar publication which the Methodist Episcopal Church began publishing in St. Petersburg, Russia, in 1909. This is not surprising, since N. J. Pöysti, who was now working for the MECS in Harbin, had previously assisted the MEC Mission in St. Petersburg. Hence, one finds in the Harbin *Khristianski Pobornik* some of the same articles which originally appeared in St. Petersburg. The Mission published 1,000 copies of *The Christian Advocate* each month for distribution.

The 1923 report of the Annual Meeting of the Mission stated that the Rev. Pöysti had procured copies of the hymnbook used by the MEC in Europe.[30] One thousand copies were reprinted for use in the Siberia-Manchuria Mission. In addition, *The Doctrines and Discipline of the Methodist Episcopal Church, South* had been translated into Russian.

On the next page there is an example of a cover page of an issue of the *Khristianski Pobornik* published in Harbin.

---

[28] *Minutes of the Annual Meeting of the Siberia-Manchuria Mission (Russian Department) of the Methodist Episcopal Church, South* (Harbin, Sept. 24, 1924), p. 31.

[29] Ibid., p. 34.

[30] This writer assumes that this was a hymnbook which George A. Simons had published in 1913 for use by the Russia mission of the Methodist Episcopal Church in Russia proper. It consisted of 100 western hymns translated into Russian.

МЕТОДИСТСКІЙ ХРИСТІАНСКІЙ ПОБОРНИКЪ

| Томъ 2 | 1-го Сентября 1924 г. | № 9 |

«Дайте мнѣ сто проповѣдниковъ, которые бы не боялись ничего, кромѣ грѣха и которые бы не желали ничего, кромѣ Бога, и я не буду безпокоиться о томъ, священнослужители ли они или просто міряне. Такіе проповѣдники потрясутъ врата ада и устроятъ Царство Небесное на землѣ».

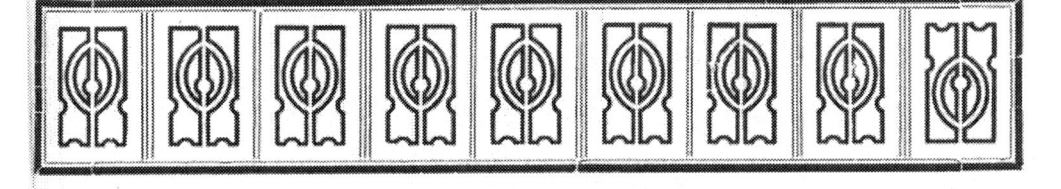

Джонъ Веслей

By 1925 the Mission had published in Russian 3,000 copies of a booklet titled "What Every Methodist Ought to Know." However, the most significant publication of 1925 was the hymnbook *Songs of Zion* with texts and music. Below is the title as it appeared on the first page

ПѢСНИ СІОНА

для

Евангельскихъ Христіанъ

and cover of the hymnbook. This was an extraordinary book, for it not only included musical settings of hymns well known among the congregations of the MECS; it included many indigenous Russian melodies and texts and translations by the significant twentieth-century Russian Protestant hymn-writer, Ivan Stepanovitch Prochanov. No other Methodist hymnal of the period included as much indigenous material that expanded Methodist repertory beyond the known hymns of western Protestantism.

The hymnal was uniquely Methodist, for its concluding section of worship resources included the Lord's Prayer, the Apostles' Creed, and Responsive Readings from the Psalms and the New Testament. While the hymnal included numerous hymns which the MECS churches in the U.S. would have customarily sung from *The Cokesbury Worship Hymnal* and the official hymnal of the MECS, it included, as noted, many indigenous Russian melodies and hymns by Prochanov. Alongside popular gospel hymns by Fanny Crosby, William Bradbury, Ira Sankey, P. P. Bliss, and others, one finds the music of Mozart, Haydn, and Bortniansky. Russian translations of hymns by Charles Wesley, such as "O for a thousand tongues to sing," "Hark, the herald angels sing," and "Jesus, Lover of my soul," were also included.

Songs of Zion concluded with an indigenous Russian hymn "Bozhe nash spaceetyel," whose chorus pleads "Spasi Russiyu" or "Save Russia."

In 1927, the publication, *Khristianski Pobornik,* was replaced by *Metodist (The Bulletin of the Siberia-Manchuria Mission of the Methodist Episcopal Church, South)*. Below is a sample cover page of the bulletin with a picture of the missionary family of George F. Erwin. This new publication was a distinct departure from the *Khristianski Pobornik,* which had included primarily Russian translations from other papers and books. The *Metodist,* however, included a wealth of material written by indigenous Russians.

МЕТОДИСТ

Издание Русской Методистской Еп. Церкви Юг.
в С. Маньчжурии.

№ 12.   Іюль 1927 г.   2-й год изд.

Пастор Г. Ф. Эрвин и его семья.
Rev. Geo. F. Erwin and family.

The Closing of the Mission

One of the great tragedies of Methodist mission history was the decision to close the Siberia-Manchuria Mission in 1927, to sell all of the property, and recall all of the missionaries. As Dana L. Robert points out, "The primary mover behind the decision to terminate was Bishop William N. Ainsworth, who succeeded Bishop Boaz as missionary bishop over the Far East. Both converts and missionaries recalled that in contrast to Bishops Lambuth and Boaz, Bishop Ainsworth was hostile to the mission from the beginning."[31] Whether or not this judgment is correct, he is the one who suggested to the Board of Missions that the Harbin mission be closed. Robert notes further, "A strange twist of the situation was that as a member of the South Georgia Conference, Bishop Ainsworth eliminated the mission of his own parishioners and friends."[32] The Siberia-Manchuria Mission had been a major thrust of that Conference and a primary source of the missionary personnel.

The Russian Methodists in Harbin could not comprehend the closing of the mission, and they pled with the missionaries to stay, but to no avail. The passion and commitment of these Russians for Christ and the Church was extraordinary. The impact of the closing of the mission on the Russian population was eloquently expressed in an article which appeared in the English-language newspaper, *The Harbin Daily,* on July 13, 1927:

> All of us Russians have had a chance to watch the activities of the various departments of the Mission, which were social activities, open for all who were interested in the new and important work done by the American missionaries. The progressive Russian press spoke with sympathy and a friendly feeling of all the phases of the American missionary work, which was marked with high culture, neutrality in political questions and tolerance in those of religion. Quietly, with the dignity characteristic of the American nation, the Mission conducted its work within the frames of loyal apology. The sermons of the missionaries were attended by large crowds of Russian people. The spacious prayer hall was by far insufficient to accommodate all who came to hear Pastor Stokes, and it was necessary to arrange improvised prayer meetings outdoors, on the wide grounds of the Methodist Institute. Much of what we Russians have heard from the Methodist bishops, pastors and missionaries has gone deep into our souls; "Our hearts burned," we may say, with the words of the Gospel.
>
> In the cultural and educational institutions of the Mission many hundreds of Russian citizens received education in the schools, studied English, typewriting, bookkeeping and other subjects; many needy people received medical treatment and medicine at the clinic. "The Women's Center" with the children's asylum and kindergarten, the summer resort colonies, the "bonfire" organisations for boys and girls, etc., [are] only a part of what was created by the remarkable organizing talent of Mr. Jenkins, Mr. Erwin, Miss Rumbough and other American missionaries, of whom we Russians cannot but speak a kind word. . . . [words missing]
>
> The Russian people will not forget the work of the Methodist missionaries, as they will not forget that of the American Red Cross in Siberia, the American Relief Administration in the depth of hunger-stricken Russia and the feelings of the American people towards the powers now ruling the Russian people.
>
> A Russian

The article, as noted, is signed simply "A Russian."

---

[31] *Methodism in Russia and the Baltic States: History and Renewal,* p. 81.
[32] Ibid.

As in the case of the Methodist churches in Russian Siberia, even though the Mission was officially closed, the congregations kept functioning as best they could. One of the Russian pastors who went to the US with Mrs. Erwin and her children when they left Harbin was A. F. Gavrilovchuk and his wife. We know part of the story of the ongoing life of Methodists in and around Harbin from an article he wrote that appeared in *The Missionary Voice* in January 1930. After two years in the U.S., the Gavrilovchuks returned to Harbin to resume service among the Methodists. Selected portions of the article, "Work Among the Russians in Manchuria," tell the the story well:

> After two years' absence and one month's travel we reached Harbin. Great throngs of people were at the station to meet us, asking us a great many questions. It was natural, of course, for them to do so. They were anxious to know whether the Methodist Church would discontinue its work, or develop it further. Besides the questions concerning our work, it was interesting to note questions about Christianity in America, whether American Christians are better than those at home, etc.
>
> We found that in the past two years Manchuria had been growing rapidly, especially the city of Harbin. Over three thousand new buildings had been erected, and a great many more were under construction. Many new offices and institutions had been opened. Harbin has become an important international center of the Far East. Over 100,000 Russians live in Harbin alone. The reconstruction of the country has brought great throngs of people here, and a great migration is taking place, hundreds of thousands of Chinese migrating from the south to Manchuria annually. The coming of a million more souls in the past eighteen months from the war, famine, and bandit areas is regarded as the greatest movement of people in modern times. All this taken together points to a great future for North and South Manchuria.
>
> Due to the unstable value of the Chinese currency, and the past wars, the economic condition cannot be said to be the best. Economic pressure is evident here, as it is everywhere present. Wages are small. The life of the European working man is not easy, due to the great competition of Chinese labor.
>
> . . . A day hardly passes in which someone does not commit suicide. There are days when several people will cut off their lives because they are not able to struggle any longer. Almost all of them leave behind the message that there is nothing to live for. White slavery, houses of shame, drunkenness, dope—all are common things, and added to the lack of knowledge of the true Christ, are contributing to this degradation and death.
>
> The condition of children is no better. It is pitiful. There are as many homeless children as there are benches in the gardens. Great numbers of them are found all over the country. They walk around the streets—ragged and hungry with no prospect of a future.
>
> Russians, young and old, men and women, need Christ. The solution of the conditions that exist here is only this—one Christ and one Gospel. People need help now as never before. It is the duty of the Christian church to come to their rescue.
>
> For several years, while missionaries were in the field, we were able to meet at least part of the need. We answered as many calls as we could. Two years ago, while the cry for help increased, while the longing for Christ was developing, we had to close our Mission. This brought upon us all the criticism of our enemies. We were looked upon as being "thrown out" by the Methodists. Now we are compelled to use basements, where it is damp and cold. We have to be without literature and good halls for preaching. We have no missionary in the field. And while we were decreasing, the cry for help increased very rapidly.
>
> But even under such conditions our people have withstood all mocking and have made some progress. God has blessed the preaching of his word in a special way. The four churches along the thousand miles of territory are improving, and the work as a whole has gone forward in a gratifying way. The general outlook for the future is bright.
>
> The churches have carried on evangelism, the Gospel being preached in halls, in homes, and in other places wherever it was possible to do so. Personal evangelism had a great place in our work. Quite a

number of people were accepted into communion with God, and there is indication of a number yet to be received.

The League for the Protection of Children took care of a great number of homeless boys and girls, but they have had to let them go back to their wandering on account of the lack of funds. The churches have tried to distribute what little literature they possessed. People are so anxious to get the literature. They are tired of atheistic, sophistic literature, and want something higher. They want the Gospel.

The church in Manchuli, which is on the border line of Russia, does great work. A great many requests come from preachers for literature. People come from Russia, begging for religion. Among the hundreds of calls we are able to answer but a few. Once we gave them several Bibles. When these Bibles reached their destination, the people divided the sixty-six books into portions, so that as many as possible might share in them. What a need! What a cry for help! What a hunger!

There are requests for aid in Manchuria itself, and from several other places, as from Jalainor, Zaton, etc. We are not able to open preaching places because we cannot furnish $400 a year to each place. We are requested to come to different towns to preach, but we have not the means to travel. We need a missionary, and workers among the women. We have three trained native girls, but we are not able to take them on full time, for we cannot get the support of $10 a month for each of them.

I write this with a feeling of sadness and disappointment that more cannot be done from a human standpoint, for "How can they hear without a preacher?" This, our immediate field of a vast number of people, of 300,000 Russians, is woefully neglected, though it is one of our most promising fields. What a pity it is that these needs and openings cannot be met in a larger way, and that the missionary cannot be had. Our hope and prayer is that God will move his people soon to answer the call for help, and that there will be some way provided to furnish us with funds and a missionary to carry forward this work in a larger way.[33]

In the above article Gavrilovchuk mentions the MECS congregation in the city of Manchuli, which was located on the Trans-Siberian Railroad in the corner of Manchuria between Mongolia and Siberia. It was very near the Russian border and, as the article by Gavrilovchuk notes, it is "the most distant congregation of our Church." It was served by the Rev. Gregory I. Yasinitsky.

Dana L. Robert relates some interesting aspects of Yasinitsky's background.

The first Bible Institute [Harbin] graduate ordained by the mission was Gregory Yasinitsky, who had fought for Russia during World War I and then was imprisoned by the Bolsheviks for refusing to join them. Though sentenced to death, Yasinitsky was freed by Czech forces who revolted in Siberia. Yasinitsky joined the White Army under Admiral Kolchak. After being deceived by Bolsheviks into a fake truce, 126 officers of Yasinitsky's regiment were bayoneted and thrown into the Hoy River. One of the few survivors of the massacre, Yasinitsky fled to Harbin and became an early convert of the mission. Raised in Ukraine as a *Stunde,* or Moravian, Yasinitsky was already a Protestant and so was put in charge of teaching the Bible in the Methodist schools.[34]

The Rev. Yasinitsky continued serving the congregation in Manchuli until 1940, when the political situation became untenable. He and his family then went to the U.S. After completing studies at the Pacific School of Religion, he became a member of the California-Nevada Annual Conference and served there until his retirement. He authored a number of books which were published in Russian in San Francisco.

---

[33] *The Missionary Voice,* January (1930): 12–13.
[34] Quoted in *Methodism in Russia and the Baltic States: History and Renewal,* p. 77.

*MECS congregation in Manchuli, China, on the Russian
border served by the Rev. G. I. Yasinitsky*

Another individual, about whom not much is known, is V. N. Pestrikoff. After the missionaries were withdrawn from Russian Siberia and moved to Harbin, Pestrikoff took charge of the work in Vladivostok. He also provides an interesting link between Vladivostok and Harbin. His wife was able to be present at the Second Annual Meeting of the Russian Department of the Siberia Mission of the MECS at its meeting in Harbin on September 11, 1923, and brought her husband's report, because he was not allowed to attend. The Pestrikoffs were apparently well educated Russians and she was elected secretary of the Annual Meeting of the Mission. Mr. Pestrikoff's complete report to the Annual Meeting is included below, for it expresses the deep commitment and hope of the Methodist communities of Russian Siberia who were facing extremely difficult times.

V. N. Pestrikoff

Report of V. N. Pestrikoff

This year the churches of the Russian Far East have had to work under new conditions. After the Far Eastern Provinces united with Soviet Russia. the conditions of life and the work of the Church were changed. New laws were made concerning church work. These laws restricted the freedom of religious work and made it almost impossible to organize new religious societies. The publishing of religious literature was forbidden and no newspaper would accept church notices.

Under such conditions the Methodist Episcopal Church, South started work for Russians in Siberia.

In Oct. 1922, Rev. G. F. Erwin organized a Russian Methodist Church in Vladivostok, Siberia. Mr. Erwin worked only a short time and was transferred to Harbin. After he moved, Mr. Taylor, missionary to the Koreans in Siberia, had charge of the work. Under his leadership the work continued to grow. The room which was rented for the services soon became too small and a larger place was rented.

Besides the religious work, evening classes in English were organized. Two Russians were employed to help Mr. Taylor with these classes.

In May the little society was sorry to learn of the departure of Mr. Taylor for America. Many thought that this would put a stop to the work and that the work in Vladivostok would be discontinued. When Mr. Taylor left, the average attendance was about twenty-five at the church services and about fifty students in the English classes.

After his departure, the regular services were replaced by weekly talks, reading of the Bible, and singing of hymns. Soon afterwards Mr. Puzankoff was engaged to hold meetings regularly. Our small choir helped as much as it could. In May and June our work was more or less a regular work and attracted the interest of outsiders, but in July, when the new laws were enforced, our work had to be stopped. Then came the difficult part of the work—to secure a juridical standing for our young organization. Since it was difficult for the old churches to obtain a right to continue their work, you can imagine how much more difficult it was to get permission for a young church. During the time when the decrees were enforced, when the property was transferred and contracts signed with the government, we could not develop our work on account of danger of being persecuted, but our meetings continued to take place. The attendance was reduced to an average twelve.

Finally, in the middle of August, after six weeks of trouble, our fundamental purpose—the legalization of the church—was reached and before us lay a wide field which was in need of a good sower.

Again we had to face difficulties. Mr. Puzankoff resigned. This resignation was very unexpected, but we did our best to keep our work going.

The English classes were continued after the departure of Mr. Taylor. In summer the number of students decreased owing to the fact that some went to the country on vacation. A few days ago we had to stop the classes until we can secure a license for our class work. As soon as this arrangement can be made we shall resume this work.

Very little relief work has been done because of lack of funds. The total spent from May to October is sixty rubles.

With hope and faith in God we look into the future. We think that we are pursuing the right course and that the first thorns and obstacles of our path only encourage us more and the seed which were sown by Mr. Erwin and Mr. Taylor will bring a good harvest. The work is greatly handicapped and further development almost impossible because of the absence of a pastor. It is desirable to have somebody who is authorized to lead the services and administer sacraments; we could do charity work among the poor people and extend our work beyond Vladivostok.[35]

---

[35] "Report of V. N. Pestrikoff," *Minutes of the Second Annual Meeting of the Russian Department, Siberia Mission of the Methodist Episcopal Church, South* (Harbin, China, Sept. 11, 1923), pp. 18, 20–21.

Epilogue

Unquestionably the mission of the MEC in Russia and the Baltic States was a promising endeavor. In Russia proper it survived in St. Petersburg until 1931, but afterwards disappeared. Even though there had been capable young candidates for indigenous ministry, the circumstances of trying to maintain a faith community under communism and train leadership was incredibly difficult. In the Baltic States Methodism had hope-filled beginnings, but the Soviet takeover obliterated it in Lithuania and Latvia, and only in Estonia would Methodism miraculously survive, though only through internal, indigenous leadership. Access to an episcopal leader was impossible.

One must remember, however, that at the outset of the missions in Russia and the Baltic States, as well as in Russian Siberia and in Chinese Manchuria, Methodism was still divided in the US. The former mission was the program of the Methodist Episcopal Church and the latter the program of the Methodist Episcopal Church, South.

We have seen in the course of this volume, however, that there was contact, if only indirectly, between the MEC Mission of St. Petersburg and the MECS Siberia-Manchuria Mission. For example, the Rev. N. J. Pöysti worked for both missions and published articles of the St. Petersburg *Khristianski Pobornik* in the periodical of the same name in Harbin.

It is not surprising that the work of the church in mission made the vision of unity clearer. In a 1924 issue of the periodical *Methodism in Russia, Latvia, Lithuania, and Estonia* some sentences beneath the pictures of three bishops, two from the MEC and one from the MECS, expressed the hope of this unity.

Bishop William Burt   *Bishop John Nuelsen*   *Bishop W. B. Beauchamp*

The passage under the photos reads as follows:

> It was under Bishop Burt's far-seeing and inspiring leadership that the Methodist work in Russia was officially inaugurated. He despised not the day of small beginnings. In 1912 he was succeeded by Bishop Nuelsen who has had the joy of seeing this Mission develop in spite of the many harassing kaleidoscopic vicissitudes of the Great War and Revolutions. Note this remarkable result: Our Russian work is now in six countries—Russia, Estonia, Latvia, Lithuania, Poland, and Ukraine! It is in the latter two countries that the great hearted, statesmanlike Bishop W. B. Beauchamp of the Methodist Episcopal Church, South has been laying deep foundations. God hasten the day when the two Methodisms shall be one![36]

---

[36] *Methodism in Russia, Latvia, Lithuania, and Estonia* (April, May, June 1924), p. 8.

To the forward-looking comment in the periodical it should be added that the opening of the Siberia-Manchuria Mission was due largely to the vision of the MECS Bishop Walter R. Lambuth.

The MECS did have work in Poland among ethnic White Russians (see Appendix 4 below) and outreach also in Ukraine. The surviving congregations in Kamenic and Uzhgorod have been mentioned. To what extent, however, one may speak of the mission in Ukraine as indigenous Russian work is another matter.

Finally, it is a tribute to the amazing faithfulness of Sister Anna Eklund and her assistant, Oskar Pöld, that the congregations in and around St. Petersburg were kept functioning until 1931. One must also pay due homage to the faithful Koreans and Russians in Russian Siberia who continued the work of their faith communities under dire circumstances until 1929, as the surviving records make clear, though all missionaries had departed by 1923. It is also a reality yet to be duly honored in Methodist history that, even though the MECS Russia-Siberian Mission was already closed, the Rev. Alexander Gavrilovchuk, after two years in the U.S. (1927–1929), returned to Harbin to minister among the Methodist Russians and that the Rev. Gregory I. Yasinitsky continued serving as pastor of the MECS Russian-speaking congregation in Manchuli, China, until 1940, when he finally came to America with his family.

Unity would come to the three large branches of Methodism in 1939: the Methodist Episcopal Church, the Methodist Episcopal Church, South, and the Methodist Protestant Church; however, Methodism in Russia would not be revived until five decades later, though never again in Harbin.

Appendix 1
Biographical Statements of the Bishops of the Missions

Photographs and brief biographies of the bishops who oversaw the missions of the Methodist Episcopal Church in Russia and the Baltic States, and of the Methodist Episcopal Church, South, in Russian Siberia and among Russians in China appear below.

A. The Methodist Episcopal Church

William Burt (1852–1936) was born in England at Padstow of Cornwall, but went to America for his university studies. He became a member of the New York East Annual Conference of the Methodist Episcopal Church in 1881. As a young pastor he went as a missionary to Italy. After his election as bishop, he was assigned to Europe and moved to Zürich, Switzerland. From 1904 to 1912, Burt's episcopal oversight included the work of the MEC in Russia, and Central and Eastern Europe.

Bishop Burt was the episcopal leader who organized the Russia Mission and in 1907 commissioned the Rev. George A. Simons (1874–1952) to go to St. Petersburg, Russia, during the last years of the reign of Czar Nicholas II to become the superintendent and treasurer of the Russia and Finland Mission. In 1912 Burt returned to the U.S., where he worked until his retirement in 1924. He died in 1936 at Clifton Springs, New York.

John Louis Nuelsen (1867–1946) was born in Zürich, Switzerland. His father Heinrich served as a pastor in the *bischöfliche methodistische Kirche* (MEC) of Germany, where young John attended schools in Karlsruhe and Bremen. Thereafter he went to the US, to study theology at The Theological School of Drew University. After the completion of his studies, like his father before him, he joined the German Conference of the MEC and continued theological studies in Berlin and Halle. Returning to the U.S., he taught theology at Central Wesleyan College in Wattenton, Missouri, for nine years before being elected bishop.

Bishop Nuelsen supervised the work of the MEC in Russia and the Baltic States from 1912 to 1924 and 1926 to 1927. His publications and papers are an important source of information on early Russian Methodism. He died in 1946 at Cincinnati, Ohio.

Anton Bast (1867–1937) was born in Denmark in the town of Løkken. After theological education, he was ordained deacon in 1892 and elder in 1894 and became a member of the Danish Annual Conference of the MEC. He served as pastor of the Jerusalem ME Church in Copenhagen from 1906–1920, when he was elected bishop.

Bast was assigned episcopal oversight of the Scandinavian countries, Russia, and the Baltic States. He presided over the 1924 Annual Conference convened in Kuressaare, Estonia, when it was renamed the Baltic and Slavic Mission Conference. He served that episcopal area, however, only from 1924 to 1925. Bishop Bast, while known as a priest of the poor and a man of a warmed heart, because of accusations of financial impropriety of which he was eventually exonerated, was removed from the office of bishop in 1928. Bast died in 1937 at Copenhagen.

Ernest Gladstone Richardson (1874–1947) was born on the Caribbean island of St. Vincent, in the British West Indies. He grew up in a Methodist home, his father being a Methodist clergyman. In 1890 Richardson emigrated to the U.S. and pursued studies for the ministry. He was ordained elder in 1896 and joined the New York East Annual Conference, where he made the acquaintance of the Rev. George A. Simons, who would become the first superintendent of the Methodist-Finland Mission stationed in St. Petersburg, Russia.

Bishop Richardson presided over the second conference of the BSMC in Liepaja, Latvia, in July 1925. It was an extraordinary meeting, for the bishop ordained nine deacons and seven elders, and consecrated five deaconesses.

He served as the bishop of the BSMC for only one year, 1925 to 1926. Richardson died in 1947 at Philadelphia, Pennsylvania.

Edgar Blake (1869–1943) was born in Gorham, Maine. His theological training was at Boston University School of Theology, from which he graduated in 1898. From 1908 to 1920, Blake was very involved with Sunday Schools and was elected secretary of the Board of Sunday Schools of the MEC.

After his election as bishop, he was assigned to the Paris episcopal area, where he served for eight years. He became well known for effective evangelistic work in Europe.

Blake presided over the BSMC which was held September 7–11, 1927, in Riga, Latvia, and which celebrated the Rev. George A. Simons' twenty years of service as superintendent.

Bishop Blake retired to Coral Gables, Florida, in 1940, where he died in 1943.

Raymond J. Wade (1875–1970) was born in La Grange, Indiana. His undergraduate collegiate studies were at DePauw University. After accepting a call to ministry and completion of the requirements for ordination, he became a member of the North Indiana Annual Conference of the MEC, in which he served as a pastor and district superintendent. He acquired considerable administrative experience as the secretary of the MEC General Conference from 1920 to 1928. Wade also served as the president of the University of Scandinavia's School of Theology in Gothenburg, Sweden.

He was elected bishop of the MEC in 1928 and assigned to the Stockholm Area of Northern Europe, which included Portugal, Spain, France, Algeria, Tunisia, the Scandinavian countries, the Baltic States, and Russia.

After the Russian invasion of the Baltics and the demise of the BSMC, which held its last meeting in 1939 with Bishop Wade presiding, he was assigned in 1940 to the Detroit Area of The Methodist Church, where he served until he retired in 1948. He died in St. Petersburg, Florida, in January 1970.

B. The Methodist Episcopal Church, South

Walter Russell Lambuth (1854–1921) was born in Shanghai, China, to Methodist missionary parents.

He was sent to the U.S. to receive his early education in Tennessee and Mississippi, where he resided with relatives.

Lambuth attended Emory and Henry College, from which he graduated in 1875. Thereafter he attended Vanderbilt University in Nashville, Tennessee, from which he received graduate degrees in theology and medicine.

After his ordination as elder and acceptance into membership of the Tennessee Annual Conference of the MECS, he returned with his wife to China in 1877, as a medical missionary.

Lambuth later served as the General Secretary of the Board of Missions of the MECS and was elected a bishop of the MECS in 1911. In the course of his eleven years as bishop he was assigned episcopal oversight of Brazil, and helped initiate MECS missions in the Belgian Congo, Belgium, Poland, Czechoslovakia, and Russian Siberia.

Bishop Lambuth died in 1921 in Yokohama, Japan.

Bishop Hiram Abiff Boaz (1866–1962) was born in Murray, Kentucky. When he was seven years old his family moved to Texas. He graduated from the Sam Houston Normal Institute, which became Sam Houston State University. He then attended Southwestern University, from which he received B.S. and M.A. degrees. He was ordained an elder in the MECS and served churches in Forth Worth, Abilene, and Dublin.

As president of Polytechnic College, which became Texas Wesleyan University, in Forth Worth, and as vice president and president of Southern Methodist University, Boaz developed a distinguished career as a college administrator.

He was elected to the episcopacy of the MECS in 1922, and was assigned to the Far East jurisdiction over the Siberia-Manchuria Mission, in which capacity he served from 1922 to 1925. After returning to the U.S., he was appointed to annual conferences in Arkansas, Oklahoma, Texas, and New Mexico. Bishop Boaz retired at the last General Conference of the MECS in 1938. Thereafter he lived in Dallas, Texas, until his death in 1962.

Bishop William Newman Ainsworth (1872–1942) was born in Camilla, Georgia. In 1891 he graduated from Emory College and after meeting the requirements for ordination as deacon and elder, he was admitted into membership of the South Georgia Annual Conference.

In 1918 he was elected bishop of the MECS and served in that capacity until his retirement in 1938. His episcopal oversight included annual conferences in Texas, Mississippi, Alabama, Tennessee, Virginia, and Georgia, and also MECS missions in Cuba, China, Japan, and Korea.

Bishop Ainsworth had episcopal jurisdiction over the Siberia-Manchuria Mission from 1926 to 1927, and it was he who endorsed and recommended its closing, which was approved by the Board of Missions of the MECS in 1927 and implemented that year. He died in July 1942.

Appendix 2

Gallery of Additional Photos from the Missions
A. The Methodist Episcopal Church

The Rev. George A. Simons with St. Petersburg Methodists

The Rev. George A. Simons and the Rev. Heinrich Holzschuher, District Superintendent of the MEC Latvia District

The Rev. Hjalmar Salmi, first ordained elder assigned as MEC pastor to St. Petersburg

One of the first Official Boards of the MECS of Kybartai/Virbalis, Lithuania, with the Rev. Rudolf Brennheiser (center)

MEC Sunday School Class Kybartai-Virbalis, Lithuania

The Rev. Rudolf Brennheiser and family, pastor in Kaunas, Lithuania. Brennheiser was fluent in Russian and preached in St. Petersburg, Russia, while Dr. Simons was on leave in Edinburgh, Scotland.

Delegates to a Temperance Conference in Tartu, Estonia
Front row, left to right: Hans Söte, Hjalmar Salmi, unknown, George A. Simons,
Orthodox priest, the Rev. Pavel Gorskoff, unknown

Architect's drawing of Riga First MEC and adjacent Orphanage, Latvia

Left: *Members of the MEC in Liepaja, Latvia, preparing wood to save heating costs for the church and parsonage during the winter*

Left: *MEC Church building in Liepaja, Latvia*

First Epworth League in Imperial Russia, Kaunas, Lithuania

B. The Methodist Episcopal Church, South, Siberia-Manchuria Mission

MECS Mission building complex, Nikolsk-Ussurisk, Russia

Completed building of The Methodist Institute of the MECS in Harbin, China

Doctors, Dentists, Nurses of the MECS Medical Clinic, Central Church, Harbin, China

*The Rev. J. S. Ryang,
Superintendent of Korean Work
Manchuria District*

*The Rev. W. G. Cram,
Superintendent of the Siberia-
Manchuria Mission*

Missionaries, the Rev. J. O. J. Taylor, wife, and children

Missionaries, Professor H. W. Jenkins, wife, and children

*The Rev. George F. Erwin and the Rev. J. O. J. Taylor
with three of the first indigenous Russian pastors in Harbin*

Bishop Boaz, missionaries, and Russian pastors
Left to right, first row: George F. Erwin, Bishop Boaz, H. W. Jenkins
Second row, Russian pastors: B. M. Venogradoff, N. J. Pöysti, G. I. Yasinitsky

First Session of the Siberia-Manchuria Mission
Bishop Lambuth (seated center), W. G. Cram (right of Lambuth), J. O. J. Taylor
(left of Lambuth), J. S. Ryang (end of first row, left), and delegates

Faculty of the first Bible Conference, Siberia-Manchuria Mission

Preachers of the Vladivostok District

First Preachers Institute, Nikolsk-Ussurisk, with the Rev. J. S. Ryang, seated center of second row

*Russian students of the MECS Bible Institute in Harbin
with Pastor Guroff (center of seated row)*

*Bishop Boaz and the Rev. J. S. Ryang (both in the first row) at the Fourth Annual Meeting
of the Siberia-Manchuria Mission with Korean Methodist Pastors*

Building in Nikolsk-Ussurisk, which was the MECS Church, as photographed by this author in 1995, see pp. 47, 85.

Building in Nikolsk-Ussurisk, which was part of the MECS Mission complex, as photographed by this author in 1995, see pp. 47, 85.

MECS Siberia Manchuria Mission Gathering in Harbin[37]

Crowd gathered at MECS Headquarters in Harbin

---

[37] The Chinese words on the front of the building read: *Ciduchiao* (Protestant) *Wei She Li* (Wesley) *Dang* (Church).

In Far-Away Siberia

A Typical Russian Family in Siberia

Appendix 3
Additional Photos of Students Preparing for Ministry

It has occasionally been maintained that the reason for the demise of Methodism in Russia proper and Russian Siberia, as well as among the Russian emigrant communities of China, was that the foreign missionaries, George A. Simons and Anna Eklund of the MEC, and the Rev. and Mrs. George F. Erwin, the Rev. and Mrs. J. O. J. Taylor, Professor and Mrs. H. W. Jenkins, Miss Constance Rumbough, Miss Lillian Wahl, and Miss Sallie Browne (assigned in evangelism) of the MECS focussed the missions too much on their own leadership and not on the empowerment and education of indigenous clergy and lay leadership. Early in his research this author shared this view to some extent. Having explored the existing available documents from the missions and the photographic material, however, this author no longer concurs in this perspective.

The mission reports are filled with information regarding the establishment of theological training institutions in Riga and Harbin. The evidence supports the fact that students from the Baltic States and Russia were also studying, and intended to study, at the MEC seminary in Germany at Frankfurt-am-Main. See the photograph below as it appeared in a 1924 MEC publication with its original caption.

Our six Russian-Baltic students at Martins' Mission Institute, Frankfurt-am-Main. Several of these desire to work in Russia.

Consider the time frame for the development of trained Russian-language ministers. The MEC was officially registered in Russia on June 12, 1909. Just eight years later in October 1917, the Bolshevik Revolution changed the course of world history. Methodism was a very young movement among indigenous Russians. Even though the MEC existed in St. Petersburg until 1931, through the heroic efforts of Deaconess Anna Eklund and the young pastor, Oskar

Pöld, and, though the MEC birthed new congregations in such places as Novgorod and Jablonitzy during this period, indigenous leadership did not survive.

It is also true that some of the candidates for ministry were of dual national backgrounds, Russian-Estonian, Russian-Lithuanian, Russian-Latvian, Russian-Finnish, etc. This did not diminish, however, their understanding of the Russian language and culture. Indeed, before the Bolshevik Revolution the major cities of Russia were prime examples of fused and mixed cultures and languages.

One reality, which no doubt greatly affected the future of Methodism in Russia, is that some of the Russian-language students at Frankfurt-am-Main would not find it possible to work as pastors in Russia after the Bolshevik Revolution.

Nevertheless, one may ask—Were there no indigenous Russian candidates for ministry? A plethora of candidates there was not. But the MEC and MECS publications of the period provide the photographs of some of these young men who had answered the call to ministry. Some have appeared earlier in this volume. Four additional photographs are included in this appendix. The first three are printed with their original captions.

Two new Russian students.

Two Russian candidates from Novgorod with their pastor, Rev. Ivan Tatarinovitch, in center.

The training of indigenous Russian pastors for the MECS congregations of Russian emigrants in Harbin (Manchuria), China, has been emphasized previously in this volume with descriptions of training, ministerial opportunities, and photographs. A portion of the moving article by the Rev. Alexander Gavrilovchuk, who returned to Harbin after the MECS Mission had been closed to continue his pastoral ministry among the Russian Methodists, has been reprinted above.

From this author's own interview with Mr. Serge Yasinitsky of San Francisco, son of the indigenous Russian MECS pastor, the Rev. Gregory I. Yasinitsky, it is clear that his father continued serving as the pastor of the Russian Methodist congregation in Manchuli, China, on the Russian border until 1940, when he finally left for the U.S. with his family because the political situation had made it impossible to continue the work.

Unfortunately we know too little of the fate of many of these Russian pastors. The histories of some of them may be lost forever. Nevertheless, the church and its scholars should honor them and their service to Christ and the church by continuing to search for information which helps complete the unknown and untold stories of their lives and ministries.

Russian students and faculty of the Methodist Training Institute with Bishop Boaz and visitors to the MECS Mission, Harbin, China

Appendix 4
The Methodist Episcopal Church, South and White Russia

The story of Methodism among ethnic White Russians is complicated and not well documented, particularly with photographs. The Treaty of Versailles (1919) granted to Poland the territory that stretches from Vilnius (Lithuania), in what would become for a time northeast Poland, to Minsk, just over the Russian border, and running south some 150 miles wide to Baranowitschi. Among the people living in this region were many White Russians. They spoke the East Slavic language of Belarus. It had been the chancery language of the grand duchy of Lithuania and became mixed with Church Slavonic, Ukrainian, and Polish. Only in the early part of the twentieth century, however, was it orthographically developed so that it could be put into an established Cyrillic form. It is not identical with the Russian language, though closely related.

In the year 1921 the MECS opened its outreach in Poland. Its work among White Russians began after 1924. While there are a few mentions of the beginnings of this aspect of the mission in the MECS periodical *The Missionary Voice*,[38] the information provided lacks detail. It is clear that the MECS mission outreach in Poland grew to include a vision of work among White Russians within the new Polish borders. There is some helpful material in the reports of the Rev. Gaither Warfield, superintendent of the MECS in Poland, as noted below.

The were four so-called "White Russian Districts" within Poland where a total of four gymnasia or high schools were located (e.g. in Vilnius and Radoszkowice), but the vast majority of White Russians had little opportunity for formal education at that time. It is reported that the MECS conducted some training institutes for White Russian teachers at the MECS orphanage and church at Klarysew, Poland, as well as in Vilnius. At this time, however, the church did not have the resources to begin an extensive educational program among White Russians.

When the Harbin MECS Mission was closed in 1927, two of the missionaries, Constance Rumbough and Sallie Browne, were reassigned to Vilnius. They assumed the direction of the MECS school for girls in Vilnius and were not directly involved with work among the White Russians.

In 1928 the Rev. Jan Witt (also known as John Witt), a Swedish Methodist, who had worked in Riga, Latvia, with the Methodist Episcopal Church, moved from Latvia to be pastor of the MECS congregation in Vilnius. Witt interested a Methodist gentleman, Ernst Nausner, who had attended school in Russia, in becoming a missionary among the White Russians. At the 1928 Conference of the MECS in Poland Nausner's application for missionary service was accepted and he moved to Sredie Sioło, a village about forty kilometers from the county seat of Wołożin. After his marriage that same year, his wife joined him in the village. They developed Methodist congregations and work in three White Russian villages: Slaboda, Srednie Sioło, and Dori. During the twelve years of their effective work a Methodist Chapel was built in Srednie Sioło. It was the only one for miles around.

Wilhelm Nausner, son of Ernst Nausner, has described the difficult village life:

---

[38] See "The Call of White Russia," *The Missionary Voice* (December 1924), pp. 5–6; "Sowing the Seed in White Russia," (August 1927), p. 14.

During Tsarist Russia school was not obligatory and there were no schools for the people. The farmers in Srednie Sioło could neither read nor write. There were no doctors, no pharmacies, no electricity, no telephone, no radio, no post office, no water pipes, no sewers, no paved streets, and no schools. One could only travel with a horse-drawn wagon or by foot. That's where I was born and grew up and as a small boy collected money for the building of the first school and, as I was seven years old, I was one of the first students in the school.[39]

In an undated report of the MECS historian, Elmer T. Clark (1886–1966) states that there are twenty MECS churches in Poland. "Four of these are at Warsaw and the others are located at the following places: Danzig, Mokotow, Klarysew, Skolimow, Lwow, Poznan, Grudziadz, Chodziez, Odolanow, Czarnylas, Katowice, Torun, Radokovitz, Vilno [Vilnius], and three other villages in the province of Little White Russia."[40] Probably Slaboda, Srednie Sioło, and Dori are the three villages to which Clark refers.

The Rev. Jan Witt served as pastor in Vilnius from 1928 to 1931, when he was followed by the Rev. Jan Piotrowski, a White Russian. Piotrowski was born in Poland and raised in the Orthodox Church and wanted to minister among his own people. As he had not learned the White Russian language well, he had to spend many long hours studying in order to be able to preach in the language. He became so proficient in it that he began publishing a small monthly paper.[41]

There was, however, other MECS work among the White Russians of Poland, as the Rev. Jan Witt reported:

The Rev. Theodore Grabinski, a White Russian exhorter, has helped wonderfully with the work in the villages around Dereczyn. He is a zealous, warm-hearted Christian, and went through many hardships with me last year (1928). Our two devoted White Russian workers, Mr. Grabinski and Mr. P. Naguj, have not dreaded any kind of trouble, but have walked from village to village either with me or without me, preaching the gospel, being urgent in season and out of season, in all kinds of weather at the very lowest remuneration. Without their cooperation, I would not have been able to reach the poor, illiterate, suspicious White Russian peasants. . . . through the work of the White Russian exhorters we have been able to get crowds of from 100 to 400 to listen to the gospel in their cottages.[42]

The conditions in the White Russian villages were extremely difficult and primitive. The Rev. Gaither Warfield described a typical meeting on the Rev. Grabinski's circuit as follows:

We arrived in the village, which was a portion of the road with long lines of thatched cottages [on] either side. Our chapel was an unfurnished, unheated room with a dirt floor. A lamp was hung by a wire to a nail in the rafter. Brother Witt announced a hymn in White Russian and by the time we had finished singing it, the place was packed. I spoke to them in broken Polish and some interpreted into White Russian and they listened most attentively. And how they begged us to come back! This is one of the twelve villages on the circuit.[43]

Clearly further research is needed regarding Methodist missions among White Russians.

---

[39] Personal communiqué from Wilhelm Nausner, December 4, 2008.

[40] Elmer T. Clark Archive 2432–5–1:42: "Czechoslovakia–Poland–Belgium." Courtesy of the Commission on Archives and History, The United Methodist Church, Drew University, Madison, NJ.

[41] From an unpublished report of the Rev. Gaither P. Warfield (missionary to Poland), Dec. 31, 1935. Courtesy of the Commission on Archives and History, The United Methodist Church, Drew University, Madison, NJ.

[42] From an unpublished "Sketch of Rev. Theodore Granbinski," p. 1. Courtesy of the Commission on Archives and History, The United Methodist Church, Drew University, Madison, NJ.

[43] Ibid.

Index of Personal Names

Ada, Sister	14, 15, 26, 28
Adeloff, Karl	25
Ainsworth, William N.	70, 80
Bärnlund brothers	1
Bahn, Ernst	34
Bast, Anton	40, 78
Beauchamp, W. B.	75
Beike, Karl	34
Blake, Edgar	42–43, 78
Bliss, P. P.	68
Boaz, Hiram A.	49–50, 54–55, 60, 62–63, 70, 80, 88, 91, 97
Böhme, Wilhelm	31
Bortniansky, Dimitri	68
Bradbury, William	68
Bradovitch, Miss	66
Brannon, L. C.	46, 52
Brennheiser, Rudolf	25, 34, 82
Browne, Sallie	95, 98
Bulgakov, A.	17
Burbulys, Kostas	35
Burt, William	8–9, 11, 14, 16, 19–20, 24, 32, 42, 75, 77
Busch, Mrs. A.	38
Carlson, Bengt A.	1, 42
Chung, Chai Duk	45–46, 52–53
Clark, Elmer T.	98–99
Cram, W. G.	45–46, 52, 86, 89
Crosby, Fanny J.	68
Datt, Vladimir	26
Dunstan, John	17
Durdis, Georg	1, 2, 13, 16, 25
Egoroff, K. D.	61, 63
Eidins, Fricis	14, 35
Eklund, Anna	12, 14, 28–29, 31–33, 37, 42, 44, 76, 95
Engels, Berta	44
Erwin, George F.	49–51, 54–55, 61–64, 69, 70–71, 74, 88, 95
Erwin, Vada	51, 54, 95
Formitschoff, Miron	30
Freiberg, Alfred	34
Gavrilovchuk, Alexander F.	61–62, 64, 71–72, 76
Gorskoff, Pavel	83
Goucher, John F.	12
Grabinski, Theodore	99
Grigorjeff, Eugene	33

Guroff, A. A.	61, 62–64, 91
Hawk, John C.	61
Haydn, F. J.	68
Heber, George	12
Hecker, Julius F.	25–26
Hecker, Olga	26
Helenius, Mrs.	24
Holzschuher, Heinrich	33–34, 81
Hübbenet, Madame de	31
Hühn, Alfred	25, 34
Ivanoff, Vladimir	26
Jenkins, H. W.	53–55, 61, 70, 87–88, 95
Joyce, Isaac Wilson	24
Kant, Jacob	34
Karlson, August	25, 28, 33
Karlson, Johannes	33
Kim, Young Hak	51, 54
Ködar, Alice	39
Kolchak, Admiral	72
Kviadravečius, Mr.	35
Kuum, Alexander	41
Kuum, Karl	13, 28, 33, 40
Lambuth, Walter Russell	45–46, 52–53, 70, 76, 79, 89
Lindborg, Karl	1
Ludwig, Paul	25
Lukas, Adelbert	26
Mändeljalg, Miss M.	39
Martinson, C.	1
Mikkoff, A.	33
Miranoff, Brother	24
Molitz, Erich von	25
Moose, J. R.	55
Mosienko, Serge	35, 36
Mozart, W. A.	68
Naamen, Mr.	49
Naguj, P.	99
Natalie, Sister	15, 26
Nausner, Erna	98
Nausner, Enrst	98
Nausner, Wilhelm	98–99
Nuelsen, John L.	27–28, 32–33, 39, 41–44, 75–77
Örnberg, K. J.	33
Parker, F. S.	53
Patjas, Samuel	33
Pestrikoff, V. N.	49, 73–74

Pestrikoff, Mrs.	73
Piotrowski, Jan	99
Plitzuwait, Peter	34
Pöld, Oskar	27–32, 40, 42, 44, 76, 96
Pöysti, N. J.	55, 61–62, 66, 75, 88
Prikask, Martin	13, 28, 33, 40
Prochanov, Ivan S.	68
Puzankoff, Mr.	74
Rafalowsky, V.	33
Ramke, Heinrich	1
Raud, E.	33
Richardson, Ernest Gladstone	78
Robert, Dana L.	70, 72
Romanoff, Tsar Nicholas II	1, 2, 77
Röandt, August	25
Röhrich, Alexander	35
Rosen, N. J.	24
Rumbough, Constance	65–66, 70, 95, 98
Ryang, J. S.	45, 52–53, 86, 89–91
Salmi, Hjalmar	9–11, 14–17, 20, 24, 26, 33, 35–36, 81, 83
Sankey, Ira	68
Schroeder, Mrs.	24
Seck, Mr. von	35
Serebriakoff, Dr.	57
Simons, George A.	11, 13–15, 17, 20, 24–37, 40–44, 68, 76, 81–83, 95
Simons, Ottilie	12, 15, 28
Skurkin, Mr.	66
Smirnov, V.	20–22
Söte, Hans	33, 35, 38–39, 83
Stokes, M. B.	45, 55
Strandross, K. U.	11
Täht, Vassili	13, 33, 40
Tartarinovitch, Ivan	29–30, 96
Taylor, J. O. J.	46, 50–52, 54, 74, 87–89, 95
Timbers, Fricis	34
Uspensky, Dr.	57
Varonen, Adam	33
Venogradoff, B. M.	55, 61, 63, 88
Volegoff, G. V.	61, 63
Volskis, Wilhelms	35
Wade, J. Raymond	79
Wahl, Lillian	65, 66, 95
Waldman, Mr.	35
Warfield, Gaither	99
Werrewkin, General	9

Wesley, Charles	17, 68
Wesley, John	17–20, 66
Witt, Jan (John)	34–35, 98–99
Yasinitsky, Gregory I.	55–56, 61–63, 72, 76, 88, 96
Yasinitsky, Serge	96

About the Author

S T Kimbrough, Jr., is a native of Alabama and is a member of the North Alabama Conference of The United Methodist Church. He holds a doctorate in Old Testament and Semitic Languages from Princeton Theological Seminary and is a graduate of Birmingham Southern College and the Divinity School of Duke University.

Dr. Kimbrough, an internationally known scholar/musician, has published over thirty books and numerous articles for leading scholarly journals on biblical, theological, liturgical, musical, and Wesleyan subjects. He has also performed and recorded widely throughout Europe, Asia, and the United States. He has served churches in Alabama, North Carolina, New Jersey, and Germany, and as Associate General Secretary for Mission Evangelism of the General Board of Global Ministries of The United Methodist Church.

Dr. Kimbrough has taught on leading theological and university faculties in the US and abroad including Princeton Theological Seminary (Princeton, NJ), New Brunswick Theological Seminary (New Brunswick, NJ), Institut für Religionswissenschaft of the Friedrich Wilhelm University of Bonn, the Illiricus Theological Faculty of Zagreb (formerly in Yugoslavia), The Theological School of Drew University (Madison, NJ), Wesley Theological Seminary (Washington, DC), and has been a member of the Center of Theological Inquiry (Princeton, NJ) since 1985. While at the Center, he organized the first international colloquium of scholars on Charles Wesley Studies and subsequently organized The Charles Wesley Society, serving as its first president.

Kimbrough's interest in early Russian Methodism goes back a number of years to his reading of the late Bishop John L. Nuelsen's history of Methodism, *Kurzgefaßte Geschichte des Methodismus* (1929), which, though revised many times unfortunately was never translated into English, except for a section that addresses Methodist beginnings in Russia, namely, chapter 10 of Part 4, "Geschichte des Methodismus auf dem europäischen Kontinent" (History of Methodism on the European Continent). Kimbrough translated this chapter into English and published it in his volume, *Methodism in Russia and the Baltic States: History and Renewal* (Abingdon Press, 1995). His research related to early Russian Methodist history has taken him to the Lithuanian National Archives in Vilnius, in Russia to the National Archives and libraries of St. Petersburg, Moscow, and Vladivostok, and to the archives of the United Methodist *Theologische Hochschule* in Reutlingen (Germany), to the Methodist Archives of Drew University (Madison, NJ), and to the archives of the Southern Europe Central Conference in Zürich, Switzerland.

Some of Kimbrough's books published as author, editor, and translator include: *The Old Testament as the Book of Christ* (1976, translation from German, Westminster Press), *Israelite Religion in Sociological Perspective* (Harrassowitz, 1978), *Lost in Wonder: The Meaning of Charles Wesley's Hymns for Today* (Upper Room Books, 1987), *Sweet Singer* (Hinshaw Music, Inc., 1987), *The Unpublished Poetry of Charles Wesley* [co-editor with Oliver A. Beckerlegge], 3 vols. (Kingswood, 1988, 1990, 1992), *Charles Wesley: Poet and Theologian* (Kingswood,

1992), *Psalms for Praise and Worship* (Abingdon, 1992), *A Song for the Poor* (GBGM, 1993), *A Heart to Praise My God* (Abingdon Press, 1996) [a commentary on the Wesley hymns in *The United Methodist Hymnal* (1989)], *Resistless Love: Christian Witness in the New Millennium* (GBGM Books, 2000), *Sister Anna Eklund, 1867–1949, A Methodist Saint in Russia* (GBGM Books, 2001), *Orthodox and Wesleyan Spirituality* (St. Vladimir's Seminary Press, 2002), *Orthodox and Wesleyan Scriptural Understanding and Practice* (St. Vladimir's Seminary Press, 2005), *Music and Mission: Toward a Theology and Practice of Global Song* (GBGMusik, 2006), *Orthodox and Wesleyan Ecclesiology* (St. Vladimir's Seminary Press, 2007).

Kimbrough has also edited numerous books of music including *Global Praise 1* (GBGMusik, 1996), *Global Praise 2* (GBGMusik, 2000), *Global Praise 3* (GBGMusik, 2004) [these three were co-edited with Carlton R. Young], and *Companion to Songbooks Global Praise 1 and Global Praise 2: Worship Leader's Guide* (GBGMusik, 2005).